SPY MOVIE: The Play!

Matthew Howell & Jack Michael Stacey

CW01497124

methuen | drama

LONDON · NEW YORK · OXFORD · NEW DELHI · SYDNEY

METHUEN DRAMA

Bloomsbury Publishing Plc, 50 Bedford Square, London, WC1B 3DP, UK
Bloomsbury Publishing Inc, 1359 Broadway, New York, NY 10018, USA
Bloomsbury Publishing Ireland, 29 Earlsfort Terrace, Dublin 2,
D02 AY28, Ireland

BLOOMSBURY, METHUEN DRAMA and the Methuen
Drama logo are trademarks of Bloomsbury Publishing Plc.

First published in Great Britain 2025

Cover design: Holly Capper

Photography by Jack Whitney

Handgun © randolph /Adobe Stock

Sticker © Ailey / Adobe Stock

Bloomsbury Publishing Plc does not have any control over, or responsibility
for, any third-party websites referred to or in this book. All internet addresses
given in this book were correct at the time of going to press. The author and
publisher regret any inconvenience caused if addresses have changed or sites
have ceased to exist, but can accept no responsibility for any such changes.

No rights in incidental music or songs contained in the work are hereby
granted and performance rights for any performance/presentation
whatsoever must be obtained from the respective copyright owners.

All rights whatsoever in this play are strictly reserved and application
for performance etc. should be made before rehearsals begin to begin to the
authors via Bloomsbury Publishing, performance.permissions@bloomsbury.
com. No performance may be given unless a licence has been obtained.

A catalogue record for this book is available from the British Library.

Library of Congress Control Number: 2025941985

ISBN: PB: 978-1-3505-8600-0
ePDF: 978-1-3505-8601-7
eBook: 978-1-3505-8602-4

Series: Modern Plays

Typeset by Mark Heslington Ltd, Scarborough, North Yorkshire
Printed and bound in Great Britain

For product safety related questions contact
productsafety@bloomsbury.com.

To find out more about our authors and books visit
www.bloomsbury.com and sign up for our newsletters.

SPY MOVIE: The Play!

by

**Matthew Howell &
Jack Michael Stacey**

Production History

SPY MOVIE: The Play! premiered at the Hope Theatre on 16 December 2023. The original cast featured:

Writer	Emily Waters
Actress	Jo Hartland
Producer	Theo Toksvig-Stewart
Stuntman	Jack Michael Stacey

The original production was directed by Matthew Howell & Jack Michael Stacey with the assistance of Antonia Salib.

The production transferred to the Old Red Lion Theatre (London) and then the Pleasance Courtyard (Edinburgh) from 25 July to 28 August 2024, as part of the Edinburgh Festival Fringe, with the following cast:

Writer	Emily Waters
Actress	Jo Hartland
Producer	Matthew Howell
Stuntman	Jack Michael Stacey and Jamie Watterson

This version was directed by Katie Ann McDonough and was subsequently selected for presentation in Warsaw by the English Theatre of Poland, with the following cast change:

Stuntman	Jamie Watterson

In 2025, *SPY MOVIE: The Play!* launched its debut UK tour, produced by Norwich Theatre in association with A. Cabbage with the following cast and creatives:

Writer	Katy Daghorn
Actress	Jo Hartland
Producer	Matthew Howell
Stuntman	Jamie Watterson

Director	Katie-Ann McDonough
Co-Director	Steph de Whalley
Designer	Caitlin Abbott
Lighting Designer	Kyle Fuller

This script was published to coincide with the production's return to the Pleasance Courtyard for the Edinburgh Fringe in 2025.

Reviews

'A deliriously fun experience that'll have you rolling around in fits of laughter.' – Country & Townhouse Magazine

Accolades

Best of the Fest – *Instafest*
Shows to See 2024 – *Edinburgh Evening News*
Recommended Show 2024 – *British Comedy Guide*
Standing Ovation Awards – *Best New Comedy (Nominee)*

Critics Say

★★★★★ *Starburst*
'Rollickingly fun and funny . . . our faces were aching with how much we were smiling.'
★★★★★ *West End Best Friend*
'Masterfully crafted silliness.'
★★★★★ *Adventures in Theatreland*
'Family-friendly . . . a must-see.'
★★★★★ *Love the Fringe*
'Funny, silly and entertaining.'
★★★★★ *Norwich Evening News*
★★★★★ *Yorkshire Times*
★★★★ *Eastern Daily Press*
★★★★ *The Wee Review*
★★★★ *Broadway Baby*
★★★★ *Broadway World*
★★★★ *Fringe Fan*
★★★★ *London Pub Theatres*
★★★★ *Fernyhough Arts*
★★★★ *Curtain Call*
★★★★ *Theatricellie*
★★★★ *Reviews Hub*
★★★★ *Good Fringe Guide*
★★★★ *Instafest*

Norwich Theatre

Norwich Theatre is a leading arts organisation in the UK and the largest in the East of England. We are deeply committed to the importance of creative experiences of all kinds for people of all backgrounds and at all stages in their lives.

We produce and present a year-round diverse programme of live performances and creative engagement activities across all art forms. More than 500,000 people a year visit our three venues, Theatre Royal, Playhouse and Stage Two in the heart of the city of Norwich. We work hard to be a place of inclusion and welcome for all those who spend time in our buildings, whether to work with us, watch a show, participate in our activities or relax in our restaurant and bars.

We are also working to put Norfolk and the East of England on the map as a place where international creativity and art are formed through our growing portfolio of originated and co-originated work and each year we increase our reach through our touring work.

Recent creative projects have included the sell-out tour of Carlos Acosta's *Nutcracker in Havana* (UK tour); Peter Brook's *Tragédie de Carmen* (Buxton International Festival); *The Land of Might Have Been* (Buxton International Festival); Carlos Acosta's *On Before* (international tour); *High Performance* (UK tour); *SPY MOVIE: The Play!* (UK tour); *Joe Tracini Needs Help* (which grew into the award-winning documentary *Me and the Voice in My Head*); in addition to our annual self-produced pantomime, one of only a handful of independently produced large-scale pantos in the UK, reaching audiences of more than 50,000 each year. We also co-commissioned Laura Horton's *Lynn Faces* alongside Theatre Royal Plymouth and New Diorama Theatre. Current and future plans include a 2025/26 tour of Carlos Acosta's *Nutcracker in Havana*; *SPY MOVIE: The Play!* at

Edinburgh Festival Fringe and on tour; *Joe Tracini: Ten Things I Hate About Me* at Edinburgh Festival Fringe; *Trouble in Tahiti* and *La voix humaine* with Buxton International Festival; and The Nimmo Twins.

Over recent years, Norwich Theatre has established itself nationally as an important supporter and developer of new musicals at the mid-scale through a commitment to early-stage investment in bold new work that both amplifies different voices and pushes the boundaries of the art form. This began with our supporting the world premiere of *SIX* at Norwich Playhouse in 2018, which has subsequently become an international phenomenon, and the burgeoning list of new musicals we have since supported and platformed includes Drew Gasparini's *We Aren't Kids Anymore*; *Cake: The Marie Antoinette Playlist*; *Police Cops: The Musical*; *My Son's a Queer (But What Can You Do?)*; *The Highway Man*; *Come Dine with Me: The Musical*; *I Wish You Well – The Gwyneth Paltrow Ski-Trial Musical*; *Silence! The Musical*. We are a member of REWRITES, a partnership programme led by The Lowry, Birmingham Hippodrome, MAST Mayflower Studios and Norwich Theatre, which showcases new musicals at the start of their journey to the stage. Through our award-winning creative engagement programmes, we also champion the power of creativity to support positive change, improve people's wellbeing and generate prosperity in all its forms.

We are a registered charity with no regular public funding and rely on a share of ticket sales, one-off grants, fundraising, sponsorship and other commercial activities to deliver our work. Any surplus funds generated each year are reinvested into our artistic and creative programmes and support our vision to achieve a positive impact in all that we do.

Follow @NorwichTheatre on Twitter

Like Norwich Theatre on facebook.com/norwichtheatre

Follow @norwichtheatre on Instagram

Norwich Theatre, Theatre Royal, Theatre Street, Norwich NR2 1RL

01603 598500

info@norwichtheatre.org

norwichtheatre.org

Registered Charity No. 262259.

A. Cabbage Productions

Comedy is tragedy plus time . . . and a joke or two.

A. Cabbage Productions is a bold new comedy company founded by writing duo Matthew Howell & Jack Michael Stacey. Known for their high-energy, inventive theatre, they specialize in smart, fast-paced comedy rooted in genre storytelling and physical chaos.

The company's name is a playful nod to the Broccoli family – producers of the James Bond films –with a comic twist.

With *SPY MOVIE* now on tour and new projects in development, A. Cabbage Productions is on a mission to shake up comedy theatre – one gloriously ridiculous set piece at a time.

cabbagealbert@gmail.com
Follow @spymovieplay on Instagram

Albert Cabbage

Albert is one of Welwyn Garden City's prominent directors, he describes himself as an auteur. His films have changed the local area, sometimes irreparably. He has produced several not Hollywood blockbusters including *You Blew up my Mother*; *Car Chase*; *Car Chase 2*, *Four Wheels are Better than None*; *Rampage at the Penguin Enclosure*; *Getting Handsy*, starring Phill Murray; *The Godfather**; *Car Chase VIII*, *Cars in Time*; *Film the Film*.

For a full list of credits you can try to find his IMDB profile.

*NB Albert Cabbage's involvement in *The Godfather* is contested.

CREATIVE TEAM

Writers: Matthew Howell & Jack Michael Stacey

Matthew is an actor, writer and director with over ten years of experience working across theatre, screen and digital audio. He is a regular cast member with Mischief Theatre and has played lead roles in several West End and International productions. He began writing sketch comedy in 2015 and co-created the duo Horrigan and Howell. Their critically acclaimed live shows have enjoyed sell out runs at the Hope theatre, Edinburgh Fringe and Pleasance, as well as garnering several award nominations and two podcast series on Audible. He has directed several short films, most recently *Lily's House* (2025). *SPY MOVIE: The Play!* is his second published work as a playwright.

Jack is an actor and writer known for his roles as Prince Edward in *Queen Charlotte: A Bridgerton Story* (Netflix, 2023) and Derek Jackson in *Outrageous* (Britbox/UKTV, 2025). His first play was shortlisted for Soho Theatre's Verity Bargate Award, and his second, *100 Paintings*, was published by Renard and enjoyed a sell-out run at the Hope Theatre.

Matthew and Jack met whilst performing in *The Play That Goes Wrong* (West End). They have written and performed together extensively, publishing their play *The New Musketeers* (2023) with Methuen Drama and starring in the UK tour of *Peter Pan Goes Wrong* (2023–2024).

Sharing a love of genre movies and fringe theatre, they wrote a sitcom pilot set in MI5, Section 13, which was longlisted for the BAFTA Rocliffe competition. After being offered a slot at the Hope Theatre, they wrote *SPY MOVIE: The Play!* and premiered it in a sell-out, critically acclaimed run under the banner of their new company, A. Cabbage Productions, named in honour of the original producers of the Bond franchise.

Director: Katie-Ann McDonough

Katie-Ann directs for both stage and screen. She was recently a participant of X-Pollinator, supported by Screen Ireland. She studied Drama and English at University College Dublin, and Theatre Directing at NUIM and on the National Theatre Studio Director's Course. She studied Script Supervision at the National Film and Television School. She is an improv facilitator with a strong background in farce, comedy and clowning. She has worked on several projects for Mischief Theatre.

Co-Director for UK tour: Steph de Whalley

Steph studied English Literature and Theatre Studies at the University of Leeds, and Acting at the Oxford School of Drama. Associate Director: *Jack and the Beanstalk* (Jordan Productions, Chatham Theatre). Assistant Director: *Wuthering Heights* (Wise Children, New York & US tour); *Peter Pan Goes Wrong* (Mischief Theatre, West End, UK tour & Latvia); *Usagi Yojimbo* (Southwark Playhouse); *Camp* (Etcetera Theatre). Co-Director: *Splinters of Light* (Edinburgh Festival Fringe). Acting credits: Anita Benn in *Doctor Who* (BBC, Disney+); *Magic Goes Wrong* (Mischief Theatre, Apollo Theatre, West End); *We're Going on a Bear Hunt* (Oxford Playhouse & Little Angel Theatre, UK tour); *How to Hide a Lion* (Polka Theatre, UK tour); *The Importance of Being Earnest* (York Mansion House, UK tour); *RIP* (King's Head Theatre); *Everything By My Side* (Lift Theatre, Southbank Centre).

Designer: Caitlin Abbott

Caitlin was a Linbury Prize finalist and RSC Assistant Designer 2019–2020, and she has twice been nominated for Off-West End Awards for Best Set Design for her work on *Houdini's Greatest Escape* (Yvonne Arnaud Theatre, King's Head Theatre) and *A Single Man* (Park Theatre). Other design credits include *My Pet Star* (Marlowe Theatre); *Wellington 24* and *Ginger Jones and the Sultan's Eye* (Theatre Royal, Bury St Edmunds); *L'Olimpiade* (Vache Baroque); *Glitch* (RABBLE Theatre); *Indigo Giant* (Komola Collective, UK tour); Roald Dahl's *Revolting Rhymes* (Opera Holland Park, Waterperry Opera Festival); *Time and Tide* (Park Theatre, Norwich Theatre Royal); *Black, el Payaso* (Arcola, Cervantes Theatre); *Crimes on Centre Court* (Theatre Royal Bath); *The Selfish Giant, Hamelin* (TRBTS, The Egg); *Sweeney Todd* (BTA, The Egg); *Autumn Opera Scenes* (Guildhall School of Music and Drama); *Perspective* (National Theatre); *Valentina Star Dreamer* (Haste/The Place); *The Mullah of Downing Street* (Chipping Norton Theatre, Warwick Arts Centre); *The Elephant Man* (Bristol Old Vic).

Lighting Designer: Kyle Fuller

Kyle is Senior Lighting Technician for Norwich Theatre. He has worked in professional theatre for many years and has supported lighting and sound across many touring productions. His lighting design credits include *The Highwayman, A Circus Carol, Joe Tracini Needs Help, The Baron in the Trees, Aladdin* and *Joe Tracini: Ten Things I Hate About Me.*

Composer: Stephen Hyde

Stephen is a multi-award-winning writer and composer of music for theatre from rural Cumbria. Hailed by *The Stage* as 'excellent, idiosyncratic and genuinely contemporary', his music draws on a diverse range of sound genres to create a highly original voice for theatre. As a composer, his work includes the pop opera *The Marriage of Kim K*; whilst as writer-composer he has created the actor-musician musicals *Robin Hood* and *The Gunpowder Plot*.

Movement Director: Jami Reid-Quarrell

Jami is stunt and movement consultant on Mischief Theatre's West End and touring productions, including *The Play That Goes Wrong*, *Peter Pan Goes Wrong* and *The Comedy About Spies*. He directed the highly cinematic and horror-inspired trailer for Opera Holland Park's production of *Lucia di Lammermoor*. Jami's eclectic client list for choreography and movement direction includes Epson, Lewis Hamilton, Ikea, Sir Trevor Nunn, The Royal Variety Performance, ITV, Depeche Mode, Satoshi Date, Casiokids, Opera Holland Park and Garsington Opera, amongst others.

CAST

Katy Daghorn – The Writer

Katy trained at Mountview. Theatre credits include Sir Henry Baskerville in *The Hound of the Baskervilles* for Theatre by the Lake/Eleanor Lloyd Productions, Mrs Hare in *Burke and Hare* for Watermill Theatre and Sandra in *The Play That Goes Wrong* (West End) for Mischief Theatre/Kenny Wax Productions and *Peter Pan Goes Wrong* (UK tour). She has also worked for Arcola Theatre, Pleasance Theatre, Theatre503 and the Young Shakespeare Company. Screen credits include feature films *Perfect State* for Deadpan Films and *Little Devil* for Clever Max Films (which won multiple awards at the Los Angeles Diversity Festival). Katy also appeared in a commercial for Expedia Las Vegas. Voiceover credits include Saltrock Surfwear for ITV West Country, Findie Ltd and BBC Radio Drama *Mind Hackers*. She is highly skilled at movement and has worked as dance captain/movement director on multiple shows. She speaks Spanish and Italian, and is a qualified translator/interpreter. She also knows basic British Sign Language (level 1).

Jo Hartland – The Actress

Jo trained as an actor at Mountview in London. Screen credits include *Casualty* (BBC); *EastEnders* (BBC); *Holby City* (BBC); *Mike* (Berlinale/Palm Springs); and *Dr Max* (Studio Soho). Theatre credits include Pleasance, The Criterion, Royal Court Theatre, Southwark Playhouse and Assembly Edinburgh.

Jo is also a writer. Her first film is currently in post-production, and she was a quarterfinalist for the Female Pilot Club's Comedy Initiative 2025.

Matthew Howell – The Producer

Matthew trained at the Mountview Academy of Theatre Arts. Theatre includes *Peter Pan Goes Wrong* (West End and UK tour); *The Play That Goes Wrong* (UK/international tour); *SPY MOVIE: The Play!* (Norwich Playhouse and UK tour); *A Sketch Too Far / Two's a Crowd* (Pleasance); *The New Musketeers* (Trinity Theatre); *Sexual Perversity in Chicago* (Upstairs at the Gatehouse); *As You Like It* (Rose Theatre Bankside); *Inigo* (White Bear). Screen credits include: Jim Dunbar in *The Real Story of Zodiac* (ITV); *Blood Witch* (Black Coppice Films); *Fright Corner* (Nina Romain); and the upcoming music video for House on Fire by ONR.

James Watterson – The Stuntman

James trained as an actor at LAMDA. His theatre credits include *SPY MOVIE: The Play!* (Pleasance Theatre); *The Play That Goes Wrong* (West End/UK tour); *Absolute Bowlocks* (A Play, A Pie & A Pint, Òran Mór); *Callisto: A Queer Epic* (Arcola Theatre/Forward Arena); *Macbeth, Titus Andronicus, Henry V* (Bard in the Botanics). TV credits include *Mrs Sidhu Investigates* (Acorn TV) and *Belgravia* (ITV). Film credits include *Man with News* (Fin Pictures); *Mercy Falls* (Magic Monkey Films); *Phones and Other Stuff* (Tall Guy Pictures); Milkrun (AJ Films); *Laurence and Olivia* (UAL).

Acknowledgements

We would like to take this opportunity to thank everyone who helped us get *SPY MOVIE: The Play!* out of our heads and into the world.

Ceri, Mir, Nic, Bardo, Rhi and everyone else at Welsh Centre, Phil Bartlett, Mark Bentley, Simon Mattacks, Liam O'Carroll, Harry Bradley, Simon Paris, Harrison Matwij, ChewBoy, Jonny Patton, Jonno and of course all of the cast and crew that have worked on the show over the years.

The fans that have supported the show so far.

And anyone else that we have missed . . . sorry, we'll buy you a drink.

SPY MOVIE: The Play!

Characters

The Writer – *MMM / Ernst Himmel / Mrs Hugs / Herr Ring / Mr Lovely / EVIW Scientist*

The Actress – *Jane Blonde*

The Stuntman – *Ian Flemish / Randy Lust / Pete*

The Producer – *Everyone else*

This breakdown is for a four-person cast, but the roles of the **Writer** *and the* **Producer** *may be split among more performers. The* **Producer** *is Albert Cabbage; other characters are unnamed and can be devised during rehearsals. In the original production, they were Ashley (***Writer***), Rose (***Actress***) and Martin (***Stuntman***).*

Notes on the Text

The film within the play is a high-octane action/spy epic like James Bond or Mission Impossible. The humour comes from the contrast between the grandeur of the story and the characters' limited resources. The charm is their relentless ambition – they don't dwell on struggles but push forward. Pacing is key; avoid lingering.

Improvised moments are marked (vamp) and may include audience interaction. '–' indicates interruption. Some interactions happen offstage, heard via microphones. Actors should create as many technical effects as possible live on stage – sound, lighting, transitions and special effects.

Firearms are mimed with hand gestures (handguns).

Important: The characters aim to create the greatest spy movie of all time, not a spoof.

Remember, no matter the scale, it will never be as big as a Hollywood movie.

Preshow

A theatre. A red velvet curtain hides the stage. As the audience enters, the **Producer** *greets them with popcorn and headshots, his aim is to encourage them to invest in the film.*

Producer (*ad libbing*)   How much are you investing today? . . . We only take cash. Excuse me, are you from Hollywood? . . . no? . . . Is there anyone important here today?

He is joined by the **Writer** *and they scope out a* **Gary** *and a* **Stagehand***.*

Producer   Hello, excuse me. It's Gary isn't it?

The **Producer** *shakes* **Gary***'s hand.*

Producer   Excuse me, sorry everyone. Before we begin I have a very important announcement. Gary is here!

Writer   All the way from Hollywood.

Producer   That's right let's have a big round of applause for Gary the big Hollywood movie producer! Gary, how much are you investing in the show tonight?

Can we get you anything Gary? Popcorn? A whiskey?

Gary everyone!

The **Writer** *and* **Producer** *then head backstage to start the show. Just as the* **Producer** *disappears behind the curtain. His head pops back out.*

Producer   Enjoy the show, Gary!

Act One

An empty stage, in the middle sits Albert Cabbage's makeshift movie theatre.

A large frame from which two theatrical curtains are draped, when opened they serve as the setting for much of the 'film's' action. Attached to the top of the frame there is a classic cinema marquee. On it in bold, black letters is advertised – 'NEW SMASH HIT SHOW SPY MOVIE THE PLAY'. There are two smaller curtains on either side that serve as further entrances. A red carpet has been laid in front of the stage.

From behind the central curtains, picked up over a microphone, we hear –

Actress Hi, Carol. No, we haven't started yet. Have you got me out of the contract or what? Look, Carol, I don't think you understand how serious this is. They want me to wear a wig!

Writer Put your phone away. We're about to start. Here we go, everyone! Break a leg!

Producer Don't let him hear you say that. It'll remind him of the accident.

Writer Oh yeah, sorry.

Stuntman It wasn't my fault.

Producer Oh, it was.

Stuntman Do you know if my Aunty Helen has arrived? It's just, she's quite important –

Producer Of course she is. Good luck, everyone!

Actress Don't say that, either! Don't you know anything about the theatre?

Producer   I know Shakespeare started in the theatre before his big break in movies. I loved Fassbender in that Scottish one –

Actress   Just don't say good luck, and definitely not –

Producer   What was it called, again?

Writer   Don't say it!

Producer   That's it. Macbeth!

Actress   No!

A music spike. Spotlight. The **Producer** *and* **Writer** *enter.*

Writer   Through the magic of cinema, you are about to witness –

Producer   The greatest spy movie ever made!

The **Producer***, in his enthusiasm, smashes the side of the frame which dislodges some of the letters on the marquee. They fall off and the ones that remain spell out 'S HIT SHOW SPY MOVIE THE PLAY'. The producer scrabbles to pick up the fallen letters.*

Writer   Due to a temporary lack of funding, this movie is, in fact, a play and my producer, Albert Cabbage –

Producer   That's me!

Writer   – has suggested some minor changes to my original script, including adjustments to the setting, casting and plot.

Producer   The trailers were my idea, too!

Writer   And that's why they've been cut. But apart from all that, everything else remains –

The **Stuntman** *pokes his head out of the curtain.*

Stuntman   Sorry, it's Jeff –

Producer   Jeff is the star of our show! Actor extraordinaire! He plays over fifty characters!

Stuntman   Yeah, has anyone seen him?

The sound of a door slamming.

Producer   Exciting news, everyone! In this evening's performance, the role of Ian Flemish will be played by the understudy!

Stuntman   Oh, excellent! Who's the understudy?

Producer   You are –

Stuntman   But, I'm the stuntman.

Writer   Isn't he brave!

There is a round of applause.

Producer   Yes, and before you ask, you've still got to do the cliffhanger stunt at the end of Act One.

Stuntman   What about the snow?

Producer   They'll do it.

*The **Producer** points at the **Stagehand**. He hands them a lanyard and some snow.*

Producer   Just throw some of this when I say snow. Got it?

*The **Stagehand** responds.*

Producer   Snow!

*The **Stagehand** throws snow.*

Producer   You're hired!

Writer   But apart from all that, everything else remains exactly –

Stuntman   And what about all of Jeff's other parts?

Writer   And in an even more exciting new announcement, our producer Albert Cabbage –

Producer   That's me!

Writer   – will be playing all the rest of Jeff's parts!

Producer   That's right, I will be playing all forty-nine of Jeff's other . . . Wait, what?

*The **Actress** enters.*

Actress   If Jeff isn't here, I am not going on.

Producer   Isn't she great . . . Gary! Hollywood's hottest new prospect, star of the Travelodge commercials, right here in . . . Where are we again?

*The **Writer** says the place they're performing.*

*The **Producer** repeats the name enthusiastically.*

Stuntman   Gary's here?

Actress   The big Hollywood movie producer?

Producer   Yes. He's right . . . there. See?

*The **Producer** points at an audience member selected to be **Gary**.*

Writer/Actress/Stuntman   Hi, Gary!

*The **Producer** shoves them offstage.*

Actress   Alright, I'll do it. But I'm still not wearing this!

*She throws the wig onstage. The **Producer** picks it up.*

Writer   So, apart from all of that, everything else remains exactly the same.

Producer   Except for the ending.

Writer   Which still definitely does not happen in space.

Producer   We'll see about that. But first, here is a word from our sponsor, Michael Mullaney's used car dealership!

Michael Mullaney's jingle plays.

Producer   So get ready for action, thrills and sex, sex, sex!

*The **Writer** glares.*

Producer   Suitable for the whole family.

Stuntman (*from behind the curtain*)   Sorry, before we start, which button sets off the big explosion at the end?

Writer   The red one.

Stuntman   Right. I'm colour-blind.

Writer   Anyway, as they say in Hollywood, Lights! Camera!

Producer   Action!

OPENING CREDITS

A rating card appears.

Voiceover   The following picture contains foul language, nudity, intense bloody violence and mild threat to life, and has been deemed suitable for children.

The rating card is certified 'U'.

Film reel SFX. Spotlight on: **Stuntman**, *as a lion, mimicking the MGM titles.*

The opening credits sequence begins. Title cards read: 'A film by Albert Cabbage / produced by Albert Cabbage / executive produced by Albert Cabbage / costume by Albert Cabbage / starring Albert Cabbage, which flips to reveal 'and some other people'. The final titles appear: 'Definitely Time to Die Again Maybe'. The **Actress** *enters as* **Jane Blonde**, *a tuxedoed brunette, and the titles circle her. She draws a handgun and fires.*

Actress   Bang!

INT. A TRAVEL BOOK BOOKSHOP IN LONDON – DAY.

Music spike. Lights up on – the **Producer** *sat in a chair as* **Danger**.

A shop bell rings, and the **Actress**, *a brunette, as* **Agent Jane Blonde** *enters.*

Danger   Welcome to my travel book bookshop in London!

Outside the window, Big Ben comes into view.

Danger   How can I help you?

Blonde   Is Harry not working today?

Danger   He's on holiday.

Blonde   He doesn't like flying.

Danger   He took a coach to Butlin's in Bognor Regis.

Blonde   He doesn't like Butlin's.

Danger   He got a good deal.

Blonde   Or Bognor Regis.

Danger   Does anyone?

Blonde   What are you reading?

Danger   It's not for sale.

Blonde   Agent Dick Hardwood in *The Spy Who Shoved Me* by Ian Flemish. Interesting book to find in a travel book bookshop . . . Colonel Danger!

She snatches the book, revealing **Danger***'s handgun.*

Blonde *slaps the gun out of his hand and knocks him out.*

Blonde   I always preferred silent reading.

She takes **Danger***'s moustache and exits.*

INT. A COOKBOOK BOOKSHOP IN EGYPT – DAY.

The **Producer***, as* **Fakesh***, is seated upright in the same position.*

Blonde *enters wearing* **Danger***'s moustache.*

Fakesh   Welcome to my cookbook bookshop in Egypt, Colonel Danger!

Outside the window, a pyramid comes into view.

Fakesh   We've been expecting you.

Blonde   That's why I always RSVP.

Fakesh   There's something different about you. You're a woman.

Blonde   Is that a problem?

Fakesh   Of course not. Our evil organisation prides itself on being inclusive to all evildoers.

Blonde   What are you reading?

Fakesh   An ancient Egyptian cookbook: owl, kheper, river Nile, pellet sign, heron, Sun disk.

Blonde   Sounds delicious.

Fakesh   There are few in our evil organisation who can read hieroglyphics, let alone cook with them.

Blonde   You read hieroglyphics beautifully.

Fakesh   I play Pictionary twice a day.

Blonde   Although, if I'm not mistaken, that doesn't say owl, kheper, river Nile, pellet sign, Heron, Sun disk. It is, in fact, kheper, River Nile, Walking Man, Bat, Sha!

Fakesh   Who are you?

Blonde *removes her moustache.*

Fakesh   Jane Blonde!

He whips out a handgun. **Blonde** *knocks it out of his hand with the book before knocking him out.*

Blonde   I've always preferred a hardback.

INT. A CHILDREN'S BOOK BOOKSHOP ON MONT BLANC – DAY.

The **Producer***, as* **Blanc***, is sitting in the same position in a tiny kids chair.* **Blonde** *re-enters wearing* **Danger***'s moustache.*

Blanc   Bonjour! Welcome to my children's book bookshop on Mont Blanc, Colonel Danger.

Outside the window, Mont Blanc comes into view.

Blanc   Now, we're just waiting for Fakesh.

Blonde *puts on* **Fakesh***'s hat.*

Blanc   Good. You're both here. Mr Lovely will be pleased. Fakesh, wait outside I'd like to have a word with Danger. Alone.

Blonde *removes* **Fakesh***'s hat.*

Blanc   Listen, Danger. We don't need Fakesh. You know what to do. Wait outside. Fakesh!

Blonde *replaces the hat and removes the moustache.*

Blanc   Listen, Fakesh. Danger has become a liability. You know what to do. Danger, you can come back in now!

Blonde *replaces the moustache.*

Blanc   Well, what are you two waiting for?

Blonde *aims two handguns towards herself . . .*

Blanc   Yes!

. . . before turning them on **Blanc***.*

Blanc   No! What are you two doing?

Blonde   Why are you all reading Agent Dick Hardwood novels?

Blanc   You could say we're big fans of the author.

Blonde   Ian Flemish?

Blanc (*in Flemish*)   *Je zou kunnen zeggen dat we grote fans zijn van de auteur.*

Blonde   Your Flemish is excellent, but I meant the author, Ian Flemish.

Blanc   Ha! If you think I'm foolish enough to tell you we've dispatched our finest evil henchman to retrieve the latest and final instalment of the Dick Hardwood series and capture its author, Ian Flemish, you are sorely mistaken. (*Pause.*) *Merde.*

Blonde   Where is Flemish?

Blanc   Northern Belgium.

Blonde   Your geographical knowledge is excellent, but I meant Ian Flemish.

Blanc   I'll never tell you he's at his home address of 23 Winchester Drive!

Blonde   Northumbria?

Blanc   That's the one. (*Pause.*) *Merde*! Who are you?

Blonde *rips off her moustache and hat and drops both onto the floor.*

Blonde   The name's Blonde, J –

Blanc   Jane Blonde?!

Blonde   Yep.

Blanc *hands* **Blonde** *the book, and she knocks him out.*

Blonde   Now, if you don't mind, I'd better run –

Skis appear.

Black run.

She exits off into the Alps. **Blanc** *looks at the disguises on the floor. He picks them up and talks to them.*

Blanc   Well, what are you two waiting for? After her!

He discards the disguises.

Blanc   *Putain*! Skis!

Skis appear. **Blanc** *exits.*

EXT. MONT BLANC – DAY.

An epic ski chase ensues. The **Stuntman** *and* **Writer** *puppet scenery and costume. They encourage the* **Stagehand** *to throw snow.*

Blonde   Ski you later, Blanc!

Blanc *tries to fire shots at* **Blonde**.

Blanc   *Merde*! I'm shooting blancs! *En garde*! *Allez*!

They fight until **Blonde** *pushes* **Blanc** *off the mountain, and his miniature falls.*

Blanc   *Sacrebleuuuuuuu*!

The miniature drops.

Blonde   He looks a little piste off.

INT. IAN FLEMISH'S HOME – NIGHT

Ian Flemish's country home. The **Stuntman**, *as* **Flemish**, *enters.*

Flemish (*writing*)   BANG! A shot rang out – and the impossible happened. The world would never believe it. Secret Agent Dick Hardwood was dead. The End.

He removes the final page.

At last. The latest and final instalment of my Agent Dick Hardwood series, entitled 'Definitely Time to Die Again Maybe', is finished. After sixty-three novels, twelve short stories and an unsuccessful foray into erotic fiction, my days as a spy novelist are over. I'm finally free to start living adventures, not just imagining them. Now, this calls for a celebration!

He reveals a box of Celebrations. He eats one.

Well, that was fun. Time for a cup of tea, I think.

He puts the stove on. There is a tapping at the window. He goes to the window and opens it. A hand is there.

What the deuce?

There is a clap of thunder, and the hand becomes a branch.

Just a branch! Nothing to be worried about.

He turns the radio on.

Radio   And in other news, millionaire philanthropist Mr Lovely has pledged . . .

Flemish *turns the dial to music. Lightning strikes.* **Mr X** *appears in the window.*

Flemish   Wait a minute . . .

He looks back, and **Mr X** *ducks out of sight, his hands in the frame.*

Flemish   Getting a bit chilly!

He closes the window on **Mr X***'s hands, as the song reaches a crescendo. He bolts up in pain, appearing to sing the note.*

Flemish *changes the radio station.*

Radio   And now, the weather forecast. Tonight there will be relentless winds, so be careful out there!

Another clap of thunder and the door bursts open, revealing **Mr X**, *picking the lock. His hat flies in, and he dives out of sight.* **Flemish** *picks it up and puts it on his desk.*

Flemish   Blasted Northumbrian winds! Better put my Chubb on.

He locks the door. **Mr X** *tries the handle.* **Flemish** *notices. It stops.*

Flemish   That wind really is relentless! I should probably call a cab if I don't want my manuscript to be ruined in the storm.

Flemish *picks up the phone and begins dialing. The doorbell rings.*

Hmm, little late for a visitor.

He sets down the phone and opens the door.

Hello? Hello?

As he exits to investigate, **Mr X** *climbs in. After a few moments* **Flemish** *reappears outside the window and* **Mr X** *ducks out of sight inside.*

Flemish Damn window!

He closes the window on **Mr X***'s hands again.* **Mr X** *screams as the kettle boils.*

Flemish Ha ha . . . Kettle's boiled!

As he re-enters, **Mr X** *struggles to remove his hands, his gloves are trapped in the window.* **Flemish** *pours himself a tea.* **Mr X** *finally gets his hands free, leaving the gloves behind.* **Flemish** *turns as* **Mr X** *hides behind the curtain.*

Flemish How strange! There's a pair of gloves in my window.

He grabs the gloves and puts them with the hat.

Now where was I, ah yes a taxi.

He grabs the phone. **Mr X** *inches towards* **Flemish** *and the manuscript. As he dials,* **Flemish** *picks up the manuscript and paces around the room.* **Mr X** *continues to try and grab it whilst getting tangled in the phone line.*

Flemish Taxi, please. What do you mean by nothing available? I'm looking out the window now!

Flemish *leans out of the window, strangling* **Mr X**.

Flemish Snow?

The **Stagehand** *throws snow.*

Flemish I can't see a solitary flake!

The **Producer** *stares at the* **Stagehand**.

Flemish *stands upright, covered in snow.*

Flemish Alright, I take that back. When can you send the next –

Mr X *cuts the phone line and ducks out of sight.*

Flemish   Hello? Hello? Damn, I've been cut off!

Mr X *ducks, struggling for breath, his hand on the receiver.*

Flemish   This bally storm!

He furiously hangs up the phone, slamming it onto **Mr X**'s *hand. He screams.*

Flemish   Wait a minute . . . forgot about my tea!

Mr X *stifles a scream and places the phone back, grabs the manuscript and hides in the closet, just as –*

Flemish   Come on, Flemish!

He downs his tea.

It's time to put the world of spies behind me. All you've got to do is get your coat on –

He opens the closet and grabs his coat.

Not this one –

He opens the closet again, and **Mr X** *hands him another coat.*

Flemish   That's better! The first thing you've got to do to write a travel book is go somewhere. Now, where is that manuscript?

Mr X *passes him the manuscript.*

Flemish   Thank you.

He puts down the manuscript and does up his coat.

Besides, a little adventure never hurt anyone.

He exits. After a moment, **Mr X** *clambers out of the closet. He grabs his hat, gloves and the manuscript. He laughs maniacally, as the door bursts open and* **Flemish** *re-enters, slamming the door in his face.*

Flemish   Well, that was a close one!

He picks up the manuscript and exits, leaving **Mr X** *knocked out.*

EXT. A DARK STREET – NIGHT.

Music accompanies the following silent sequence of lights going up and down on each pair's walking legs, like cuts in a film:
Flemish's *feet walking through the dark. After a few moments, a second set of feet appears;* **Mr X** *follows.*

Flemish *stops. So does* **Mr X**. **Flemish**'s *feet turn, and as he does,* **Mr X**'s *feet slip out of the spotlight.*

Flemish   Must be my imagination . . .

He turns again, and **Mr X** *disappears from the light.* **Flemish** *and* **Mr X** *continue walking, both building to a run.* **Mr X** *drops behind.*

Flemish   Phew! I think I lost him . . .

INT. THE OFFICES OF BOURNE PUBLISHING – DAY.

Light up on **Bourne**'s *office.* **Bourne** *is sitting at his desk.*

A buzzer goes off.

Bourne   Bourne Publishing.

Flemish (*off*)   Blimey you must be bored of it by now.

Bourne   Don't try to be funny, Flemish. You're late?

Flemish   I had cab trouble.

Bourne   That's no excuse for being tardy.

Producer   Can we say that?

Writer   It means late!

Flemish   Bourne, I've killed him.

Bourne   Good, good man! You'll be put away for this and it damn hard to write a book in jail.

Flemish   No, Bourne, I've killed Agent Dick Hardwood.

Bourne   You've killed the hero of the best-selling series we've ever had. Dammit, Flemish, I preferred it when you were a murderer.

Flemish (*off*)   Let me up, it's raining cats and dogs and gloves and hats out here and I want to tell you all about my new travel book.

Bourne   Fine, I'll buzz you in.

Flemish   The first one is going to be set in Scarborough.

Bourne   Flemish, I've said it before and I'll say it again don't try to be funny.

He buzzes him up.

Mr X *appears behind* **Bourne**. *He grabs him.*

Bourne   Ah! It was a joke. I love Scarborough. It's thrilling!

Mr X *and* **Bourne** *struggle, pressing the buzzer.* **Mr X** *gags* **Bourne***, steals his hat and hides him in the cupboard.* **Mr X***, donning the disguise, sits in* **Bourne***'s chair as* **Flemish** *enters.*

Flemish   I'm here, Bourne, and with the manuscript.

A hand emerges from behind the chair.

Not so fast, Mr Bourne. I won't hand over the final Dick Hardwood novel until you sign off on *The Extraordinary Travel Adventures of Ian Flemish.*

Mr X   Enough. The manuscript. Now. Or I'll make you pay.

Flemish   For the print run? Don't be ridiculous! (*Pause.*) How's fifty–fifty?

Mr X   The manuscript.

Flemish   Sixty-forty?

Mr X   Or else.

Flemish   Seventy–thirty?

Mr X   Mr Flemish, if you don't give me that manuscript right now, I will, actually, physically, literally, kill you – dead.

The chair spins. It is **Mr X** *in the* **Publisher**'*s place. He pulls out a knife and holds it to* **Flemish**'*s throat.*

Flemish   Talk about a cutthroat industry! Alright, alright . . .

Mr X *lowers the knife.*

Flemish   I'm willing to go to ninety-nine–one, but that's my final offer.

Mr X *goes to strike* **Flemish**.

Flemish   Wait a minute. Mr Bourne is right-handed.

Mr X *changes his grip.*

Flemish   And he's at least two feet shorter.

Mr X *shortens himself.*

Flemish   Erm – maybe one and a half.

Mr X *raises himself a little.*

Flemish   Split the difference.

Mr X *splits the difference.*

Flemish   And he has a moustache.

Mr X *puts on a moustache.*

Flemish   Oh my God. (*Pause.*) I think I left my oven on!

Mr X *launches himself as* **Jane Blonde** *bursts in.*

Blonde   You and I are going to have a falling-out.

She kicks him out of the window. He screams for a while, then hits the floor.

Flemish   How did you get in here?

Blonde   Cat flap.

Flemish   Damn pussy! You killed my publisher!

Blonde   He wasn't your publisher.

Flemish   Don't be ridiculous!

Blonde *opens the wardrobe, revealing* **Bourne**.

Flemish   Mr Bourne! What did he do to you?

Bourne   Don't worry, Flemish, this is the 1950s, I'm used to being in the closet. Jim from HR is here too!

Jim *appears, gagged.*

Jim (*muffled*)   Hello!

Blonde *closes the closet.*

Blonde   Satisfied?

Flemish   Who was that other man?

Blonde   Here's here to kill you and steal your manuscript

Flemish   Don't be ridiculous!

The buzzer goes off.

Mr X (*off*)   Let me back up, Mr Flemish! I'm not here to kill you and steal your manuscript!

Blonde   Now, are you going to come with me?

Flemish   Where are we –

Blonde   You can ask questions on the way.

Flemish   Why is he –

Blonde   You can ask questions on the way.

Flemish   I'm not going anywhere unless you tell me who you are right now!

Blonde *slaps* **Flemish**. *They lock eyes. She takes her moment.*

Blonde   The name's Blonde, J–

Mr X *appears at the window.*

Mr X   Jane Blonde!

She punches him and he falls again.

Blonde   Not all storeys have a happy ending.

Flemish   That's good, but only if it's written –

Blonde *exits.*

Flemish   When you say it, it's not clear that you mean storey with an 'ey' and –

Mr X *reappears at the window. He reaches for* **Flemish**. *He slams the window down onto his hands and* **Mr X** *falls again.*

Flemish   I guess his Friday night plans just went out the window.

Blonde *reappears.*

Blonde   Don't do that. Only I get to do that.

EXT. A COUNTRY ROAD – DAY.

Blonde *and* **Flemish** *in a car. A sign reads: 'A Road . . . in England'. They swap sides.*

The **Producer** *and* **Writer** *appear with scenery and create a sense of movement.*

Flemish   That was a close one! Where are you taking me?

Blonde   Somewhere you and that manuscript are safe.

Flemish   Do you have to drive so fast?

Blonde   There's only one way to drive this car, Flemish, and that's fast.

She accelerates, and the **Producer** *and* **Writer** *move the scenery faster.*

Blonde   She purrs like a kitten.

The **Producer** *meows.*

Blonde I think we're safe now.

Flemish Thank God, I need some air

The scenery whacks him. The car slows down.

Flemish Ow!

Blonde Don't touch anything. This isn't just a car – those buttons each control a gadget more deadly than the last. Flamethrowers, missiles, you name it.

Flemish What does this do?

Blonde Oil slick.

Flemish And this?

Blonde Parachute ejector seat.

Flemish And this?

Blonde Don't press that. It's the horn.

Flemish Don't tell me, a sonic boom?

Blonde No, it's just a horn. But this is a residential area.

Flemish Is Jane Blonde your real name?

Blonde Of course. But nobody calls me Jane because of my striking blonde hair.

Flemish It really is strikingly blonde.

Blonde The man after you is Mr X. He is a henchman for the deadliest organisation in the world: EVIW.

Flemish Evil?

Blonde EVIW. It's an acronym. Every Villain In World.

Flemish EVIW?

Blonde Yes, the founder was a cockney.

Flemish What do they want from me?

Blonde   It's your manuscript he's after. The person he works for would kill to read it. My employer is eager to get their hands on that before they do.

Flemish   Your employer?

Blonde   The Secret Service.

Flemish   The Secret Service!

Blonde   Keep your voice down! It's a secret.

Flemish   You're a spy?

SFX engine noise.

Blonde   Damn! Looks like our friend is back. Hold on.

The car swerves. Music.

Do you know how to use one of these?

She shows **Flemish** *her handgun.*

Flemish   How hard can it be?

He takes the handgun. Puts his middle finger up. **Blonde** *takes it back.*

Flemish   Sorry I'm left-handed.

Blonde   Alright, I'll shoot. Here, take the wheel.

Flemish *takes the wheel.* **Blonde** *shoots at* **Mr X**, *who avoids the bullets, the* **Writer** *making small impact explosions behind him.*

Blonde   Bang! Bang! Bang!

Flemish   He's catching up! Hold on!

He puts his foot down. They pull away.

Blonde   Flemish, it's time to give our friend the slick, oil slick.

Flemish   But you said –

Blonde   Push the button in three, two, one!

Flemish *pushes the button.* **Mr X** *sees it and wobbles but remains upright.*

Blonde   Damn. The road is too straight.

Flemish   Bloody Romans!

Blonde   Try the flamethrower.

Flemish *pushes the button.* **Mr X** *avoids a flame.*

Blonde   Blast! Missiles.

Flemish *pushes the button.* **Mr X** *avoids the missiles.*

Blonde   This guy is good. Take that right turn.

A sign appears that reads 'NO RIGHT TURN'.

Flemish   Are you sure?

Blonde   Just do it.

Flemish *swerves right. The sign flips to 'BRIDGE COLLAPSED'. They duck under it, and* **Mr X** *crashes through it.*

Blonde   He's still there.

Flemish   We're running out of road. The bridge is down!

Blonde   Quickly, push the ejector seat button.

Flemish *pushes the button. Horn!*

Blonde   The other one.

Flemish *pushes the button. The horn sounds again.*

Blonde   The other other one.

Flemish   Oh!

Mr X *grabs the manuscript. He exits.*

Flemish   No! My manuscript!

Blonde *and* **Flemish** *fly up into the air. They exit behind the curtains.*

Blonde (*off*)   Deploy your parachute!

Two toy parachute men drop from above and float to the floor.
Blonde *and* **Flemish** *re-enter and are descending to earth, lights and cars far beneath.*

Blonde   Beats the rush-hour traffic.

EXT. A PHONE BOOTH – NIGHT.

A telephone box. A **Man** *is inside.*

Man   No, you hang up. No, you hang up. No, you –

Mr X *appears.*

Man   I'll hang up.

He reaches his hand in and hangs up the call. The **Man** *exits.*

Mr X   This is Mr X. I'd like to place a call to EVIW's top-secret London HQ.

There is a noise. The phone booth spins into –

INT. EVIW HQ – NIGHT.

EVIW's London headquarters. **Mr X** *looks around for a moment.*

Mr X   Hello.

Mr Lovely *suddenly appears seated, his upper half visibly obscured behind a screen. Throughout the scene,* **Lovely** *speaks through a toy voice changer, which you can see him holding. While using the voice changer, the* **Writer** *is practically inaudible; only the shape of* **Lovely**'s *lines should come across.*

Lovely (*inaudible*)   Mr X, we've been expecting your arrival. I trust you have the manuscript.

Pause.

Mr X *doesn't understand what he is saying.*

Producer   What?

Lovely (*repeating inaudible*)   Mr X, we've been expecting your arrival. I trust you have the manuscript.

Beat.

Mr X   If you're asking whether I have the manuscript, it's right here.

Lovely (*inaudible*)   Good. And Flemish?

Beat.

Mr X   If you're asking for Flemish – he's escaped, sir.

Lovely (*inaudible*)   How did you let him?

Producer   Try a different setting!

The **Writer** *tries a different setting.*

Lovely (*inaudible*)   How did you let him escape?

Producer   How did I –

Lovely (*inaudible*)   How did you let him escape?

There is an opportunity to vamp for a few lines, until the **Producer** *has had enough.*

Producer   For God's sake. Gary can't hear a word you're saying!

The **Producer** *picks up a chalkboard.*

Writer   What are you doing?

Producer   Subtitles.

Writer   I'll just do it without this.

Producer   Don't worry, people love foreign films now. It's cultured.

The **Writer** *continues without the voice changer. The* **Writer** *has chosen to play* **Lovely** *as Scottish and uses a thick Scottish accent.*

Lovely   How did you let him escape?

Mr X   He's with somebody, sir. A spy, I think.

Lovely   Who?

Mr X   I think her name is Blonde, sir –

Lovely   Jane Blonde! I want Flemish and his manuscript. And I want Blonde dead. She has scuppered my evil plans for the last time, and she shall face the cold, hard force of my vengeance!

The **Producer** *reveals what he has written, 'A SCOTTISH ACCENT', and presents this to the audience.*

Lovely   You have failed me, Mr X. I would like you to meet a friend of mine. Oh, Mr Hugs!

Mr Hugs *(off)*   Hugs!

Lovely   There he is!

Mr X   I'm sorry, sir, it's not my fault; it was the British spy.

Lovely   There is no reason to be upset, Mr X. Why don't you give Mr Hugs a little hug?

Mr Hugs   Hugs!

Mr X   I suppose that could be quite nice.

Lovely   Oh yes, there's nothing like a hug to make one feel better.

Mr Hugs *(off)*   Hugs!

Mr X   Oh, this is lovely. Getting a little tight, though . . .

Lovely   That's it, let it all out.

Mr Hugs   Hugs.

Mr X   Actually, I'm finding it a little difficult to breathe –

Lovely   Oh, yes, Mr X. Mr Hugs's cuddles can be . . .

Mr Hugs *squeezes the life out of* **Mr X**.

Lovely   Deadly.

Mr Hugs   Hugs!

INT. MI6 HQ – DAY.

The headquarters of MI6. It is a mess.

Flemish   Wow! The British Secret Service!

Blonde *glares.*

Flemish   Sorry. (*Whispering.*) The British Secret Service!

Mr Cashless Payment *appears with a hat stand.*

Mr Cashless Payment   Agent Blonde, you're back.

Blonde   Hello, Mr Cashless Payment.

She removes her hat and tries to throw it on the hat stand. They miss. (If the actor gets it the first time, cut to 'First time every time'.)

Producer   Cut!

Writer   You can't cut in a play.

Producer   Take two!

The **Producer** *picks up the hat and gives it to the* **Actress***.*

Producer (*to* **Gary**)   I'm so sorry about this Gary.

They repeat this and the **Producer** *vamps until it lands on the hat stand. He may have to move the hat stand closer to the* **Actress***.*

Mr Cashless Payment   First time every time. You're late.

Blonde   I got into a spot of bother in Lancaster.

Mr Cashless Payment   Oh, Blonde! When are you going to take me to Lancaster?

Blonde   One day, I promise I'll take you to Lancaster.

Mr Cashless Payment *exits, swooning.*

Mr Cashless Payment   Better hurry, Blonde. MMM is expecting you.

MMM *enters.*

MMM   Blonde! Sorry about the mess. I'm doing a spot of DIY. We've got a mole. Apparently, we've got to get new fences.

Blonde   Who told you that?

MMM   The minister of defence.

The **Minister of Defence** *pops his head over the fence.*

Minister of Defence   Morning!

MMM   How was your trip?

Blonde   My plane was shot down, so I fashioned it into a wind-powered boat.

MMM   Plane sailing, then.

Blonde   Exactly.

MMM   We got your message, so I've called a general meeting of the most diverse, privately educated white male minds the British government can offer.

The following happens fast: the **Producer** *in a flurry of hats and wigs.*

MMM   Here they are. General Red.

General Red   Blonde.

MMM   General Black.

General Black   Blonde.

MMM   You know General Knowledge.

Blonde   Of course, he's on my pub quiz team.

General Knowledge   See you Tuesday, Blonde!

MMM   General Purpose.

General Purpose   Sorry, I'm late, Blonde; busy doing absolutely everything.

MMM   And General Anaesthetic.

General Anaesthetic *snores. A* **Private** *enters.*

Private   Sorry, sir – he's deep undercovers.

MMM   General Direction is also supposed to be here. Where is General Direction?

Private   Somewhere over there, I think.

MMM   This is a General Meeting. What are you doing here, Private?

Private   That's private!

MMM   Come on, Private! Or do you want me to set the Rear Admiral on you again?

MMM *spanks the* **Private***.*

Private   We've just received information about a shipment of counterfeit kitchen counters being delivered to a Russian count, whom we suspect is about to launch a counter-attack.

MMM   Who's the source?

Private   Counterintelligence.

MMM   Right, better get Special Branch on the line.

Private   Yes, sir.

Private *exits.*

MMM   Damn privates.

Blonde   Can't get the staff?

MMM   No, I've just got an itch. I'll have to tell our American friends across the pond. Oi! Yanks!

Yank   Yeehaw!

MMM   Stop feeding the ducks, and listen up. We have a situation developing, and we may need your help.

Yank   Fire the nuclear missiles!

MMM   No! Just prep the Pentagon.

Yank   Got it, catch ya later. Blonde.

Yank *exits.*

Blonde   Must be serious if you're getting the Americans involved.

A **Scottish Police Officer** *pokes his head in.*

Scottish Police Officer   Och aye, what's happening here?

MMM   Oh, nothing, officer!

Police Officer *exits.*

MMM   Damn Scotland Yard. Get that file on my desk, Pronto!

Pronto *appears.*

Agent Pronto   *Buon giorno!*

MMM   Thank you, Pronto. Now organise a wiretap.

Agent Pronto   Already on it.

Agent Pronto *taps some wire. Electrical fizz! The lights flicker.* **Pronto** *exits.*

MMM   Where's Que? Simon!

Simon *enters.*

Simon   What do you want?

MMM   Fetch Que. I need him to conduct an analysis of Flemish's book.

Simon   Don't you mean manuscript?

MMM   Manuscript.

Simon   What's the magic word?

MMM   Please.

Simon   Whatever.

He exits.

Blonde   It's unlike Simon to be so disagreeable.

MMM   Oh no, he's just been promoted to petty officer!

Private *enters with a telephone.*

Private   Special Branch on the line, sir.

Private *shows* **MMM** *a branch attached to a phone.*

MMM   Good work, Private. I'll see you in the treehouse later.

Private *exits.*

MMM   Mr Flemish, I've no doubt you have many questions concerning the nature of your being brought here.

Flemish   You can say that again.

MMM   Mr Flemish, I've no doubt you have many questions concerning the nature of your being brought here.

Flemish   Yes.

MMM   I cannot give you too many details, but we believe EVIW intends to use your latest manuscript as a mass brainwashing device.

Flemish   That's ridiculous!

MMM   Watermelon!

Flemish   What?

MMM   Watermelon!

Flemish   No, thank you. I'm not very hungry.

MMM   Damn, I thought that was the trigger word. Bad counterintelligence!

Counter-Intelligence (*off*)   Sorry, sir!

MMM   Now, all we need is your manuscript, and then you can be on your way.

Flemish   What if I don't want to give you the manuscript?

MMM   Corporal Punishment!

Corporal Punishment   Grr!

Flemish   I lost it!

Corporal Punishment   Oh . . .

Corporal Punishment *exits.*

MMM   You lost it!? The fate of the entire world is in that manuscript!

General Anxiety (*off*)   Ah!

MMM   Shut up, General Anxiety! Well, then, you'll just have to stick together.

Blonde   Are you sure that's wise, sir? I prefer to work alone.

MMM   Flemish wrote the manuscript. Without it, only he knows what it contains. Your mission, should you choose to accept it, is to track down Flemish's manuscript and foil EVIW's evil plan for global destruction, resulting in almost certain death.

Flemish   I'm not doing that!

Corporal Punishment *appears and whips the whip.*

Corporal Punishment   Grr!

Flemish   Of course I'm doing that!

Corporal Punishment   Oh . . .

MMM   Thank you, Corporal Punishment.

Corporal Punishment *exits.*

MMM   Study this face carefully. It is an artist's impression of the person we suspect is the head of EVIW.

MMM *reveals a crude drawing of* **Lovely**. *The* **Writer** *looks at it. The* **Producer** *points at the* **Stagehand**.

MMM   Did you get all of that, General Exposition?

General Exposition *enters.*

General Exposition (*in one breath*)   So you're saying that acclaimed spy novelist Ian Flemish has been brainwashed by EVIW to covertly transmit EVIW's evil plans for global destruction to all members of EVIW everywhere using the final instalment of his Dick Hardwood series entitled *Definitely Time to Die Again Maybe* and now they want to get their hands on the manuscript and kidnap Flemish before we have a chance to decode it?

MMM   You can say that again!

General Exposition   No, I can't.

General Exposition *disappears.*

MMM   Blonde, meet Que at the Ritz to collect your equipment. I'm off to see a man about a mole.

Blonde   The one in MI6?

MMM   Don't be ridiculous, Blonde. It's on my bottom.

MMM *throws* **Blonde's** *hat onto her head. Whatever happens –*

MMM   First time, every time.

MMM *exits.*

Blonde   I hope you brought your dinner jacket.

INT. THE RITZ – NIGHT.

The Ritz. A **Waiter** *enters.*

Flemish   Wow, the Ritz!

Blonde   Keep an eye out, Flemish. Que is a master of disguise.

The **Waiter** *enters with a table set for afternoon tea, a large silver cloche and a wine list at the centre.*

Blonde   Good evening, Philippe.

Waiter   Good evening, Agent Blonde. I have you sat at your usual table. Today's special is partridge; it comes highly recommended. First, though, I have prepared a special entrée. Please enjoy.

Flemish   Can I sit at the head of the table, Blonde?

Blonde   I think that seat might be taken.

*The **Waiter** lifts the cloche, revealing **Que** inside.*

Que   Sorry, Blonde. I just finished my lunch. How was your trip?

Blonde   I had to thwart an assassination attempt on the Orient Express, armed only with what I could find on the pudding trolley.

Que   Piece of cake, then.

Blonde   Exactly.

Flemish   Yes, please!

Que   Hands off, Flemish, you haven't had your partridge yet. Besides, this is a British Intelligence cake. Top secret.

Blonde   It looks like walnut to me.

Que   Pay attention, Blonde. Under this table, you'll find a suitcase with everything you'll need for your mission: inside is a mini-gun, a mini-grenade, a mini-missile, a mini-bomb and a mini-milk.

Blonde   Sounds deadly.

Que   There's nothing funny about lactose intolerance, Blonde. Just ask my wife. Speaking of lactose, Philippe, the butter dish.

*The **Waiter** presents a butter dish; he opens it, and inside is a watch.*

Que   Your new watch.

Blonde   You really know how to butter someone up.

Que Listen carefully.

Blonde I can handle a wristwatch, Que.

Que Not this one, Blonde.

Que *takes the watch from the dish using his mouth.*

Que On it, there are two dials; the first dial turns the watch into a high-powered explosive with a ten-second fuse; the second dial will emit a sonar frequency that will render anyone within earshot temporarily deaf.

Flemish This one?

Que No, don't –

Flemish *presses the watch. A foam finger presses the model.*

BEEP! Silence for a moment. **Flemish** *and* **Que** *speak, silently, until – BEEP!*

Que (*shouting*) Don't be ridiculous, Flemish. Of course, it doesn't tell the time!

Blonde But if it won't tell the time, how will I know when to return it to you?

Que I don't care when you return it to me, as long as it's in one piece.

Blonde Well, if we're done, I think it's time to clock off. Philippe.

Que Oh, grow up, Blonde.

The **Waiter** *replaces the lid.*

Producer Wait! We didn't mention the car!

The **Waiter** *lifts the lid.* **Que** *is gone and reappears behind the wine list.*

Que I didn't mention the car.

Blonde What is it this time, the Aston?

Que   No.

Blonde   The jag?

Que   No.

Blonde   The BMW?

Que   No.

Blonde   What, then?

Que   It's a top-of-the-range Hyundai i10.

Blonde   What range is that?

Que   The huge range available at Michael Mullaney's Used Car Dealership.

Michael Mullaney's jingle plays.

Blonde   Does it have –

Que   No.

Blonde   Does it have –

Que   No.

Blonde   What does it have?

Que   Zero per cent finance, around six months' MOT and a free Michael Mullaney's air freshener.

Blonde   What will you think of next?

Que   Just bring it back with a full tank of fuel. Right, better be off. I recommend the shiraz; it goes well with a bit of partridge. Goodbye, Blonde.

*The **Waiter** replaces the wine list. The **Waiter** wheels **Que** off.*

Blonde   Flemish, get some cake. I need to talk to the CIA.

EXT. TELEPHONE BOOTH – NIGHT.

Jane Blonde *is in the telephone box. A phone rings. Lights up on* **Randy Lust**.

Lust   Randy Lust, secret double agent.

Blonde   It's Blonde.

Lust   I know lots of blondes.

Blonde   And I know lots of randy spies, but let's keep this civil.

Lust   Jane Blonde, secret agent. It's good to hear your voice.

Blonde   I need information on EVIW.

Lust   Don't we all?

Blonde   You know I hate answering questions with questions.

Lust   I don't know . . . do I?

Blonde   Don't play games.

Lust   Okay. Tits for tats.

Blonde   It's tit.

Lust   Singular? What a shame. What do you know about the mole?

Blonde   The one on the inside of your thigh or the one –

Lust   The one in MI6.

Blonde   MMM is on the case. Now, tell me what you know about the manuscript.

Lust   It's on its way to Herr Ring.

Blonde   Herr Ring? Sounds fishy.

Lust   Nobody knows his secret evil identity because of an ingenious disguise, but we do know two things. One: he's a notorious gambler.

Blonde   What's the second thing?

Lust   He's allergic to walnuts. Take this –

He takes out a picture of **Himmel** *and passes it to* **Blonde**.

Lust   His name is Ernst Himmel. He's an EVIW double agent. He'll know where Herr Ring is. Find him, and you'll find your manuscript.

Blonde   Randy –

Lust   Don't tell me. I'm a bastard?

Blonde   Yes. But – thanks.

Lust   Good luck, Blonde.

She closes the shutter on him.

Blonde   I don't need luck. I'm Blonde, Jane –

Music.

Actress   Hey!

Tech Operator   Sorry!

EXT. A PARK – DAY.

A park bench. **Flemish** *enters.* **Blonde** *watches him from a distance.*

Blonde   Flemish, can you hear me?

Flemish (*touching his ear*)   Loud and clear, Blonde. Where are you?

Blonde   I'm watching from the building opposite, so don't worry. You'll be fine if you don't make a scene.

Flemish (*waving*)   Oh, there you are! Hello, Blonde!

Blonde   Stop waving. Your target is Ernst Himmel, a Swiss EVIW scientist secretly working for the CIA. He's here to meet his handler for a regular dead drop, but you'll intercept them.

Flemish   And why am I doing this?

Blonde   Because Himmel will know who I am. Remember: a briefcase, spectacles and a hat.

Ernst Himmel *enters with a briefcase, wearing spectacles and a hat. During the following, another man with a briefcase, glasses and a hat,* **Derek***, sits between them.*

Flemish   I see him.

Blonde   Just stick to the script I taught you.

Flemish   Roger.

Blonde   Who's Roger?

Flemish   No I mean Roger that.

Blonde   Don't be rude.

Flemish *sits down.*

Flemish   Lovely morning, isn't it?

Derek   Yes, quite agreeable.

Flemish *takes out a pack of cigarettes and fumbles with them.*

Flemish   Do you have a light?

Derek   No, I don't smoke.

Flemish   Really?

Derek   Yes.

Flemish   But it's the fifties.

Derek   I don't smoke.

Flemish   But those look like such lovely cigarettes you're smoking.

Derek   What are you talking about? I just told you I don't smoke.

Flemish   Do you smoke this flavour?

He flashes his packet.

Derek   How could I know that flavour when I don't smoke? Are you quite alright?

Flemish *touches his ear.*

Flemish   This isn't working, Blonde.

Blonde   Stay calm, Flemish.

Flemish   Roger.

Derek   My name isn't Roger, it's Derek.

Flemish   Well, Derek. Perhaps I might introduce you to this lovely flavour of cigarette?

Derek   Oh, I see, you're a salesman? No, thank you.

Flemish   No. I just think you might really like this cigarette if you give it a try.

Derek   Please leave me alone, or I'll report you to the police.

Flemish   Help, Blonde. Repeat: in need of assistance, Roger.

Derek   I've told you my name is Derek!

Flemish   Nice to meet you, Derek. The name's Flemish, Ian Flem –

Blonde *(off)*   No! The winter in London is . . .

Flemish   The winter in London is . . .

Derek   It's springtime.

Flemish   I know it's just.

Derek   Just what?

Blonde *(off)*   Lovely, but –

SFX radio static.

Flemish   Lovely butt!

Derek   I beg your pardon!

Flemish   Blonde, what's the next line? Blonde? I'm starting to look like an idiot here.

Derek   What did you just call me?

Flemish   No, not you, I was talking to Roger.

Derek   It's Derek!

Flemish *looks at* **Derek** *and laughs coquettishly.*

Flemish   Would you like a drink?

Derek   No, I would not like a drink. Now leave me alone, you silly little man.

Flemish   Alright. I think this is for me, so I'll just take it and be on my way.

He grabs the suitcase, but **Derek** *has it tightly in his grip.*

Derek   What on earth do you think you're doing?

Flemish *and* **Derek** *struggle over the case.*

Flemish   Backup, I need backup!

Blonde   You're cutting out, Flemish. What's happening?

Flemish   He has a rolled-up newspaper. I repeat, he is armed!

Derek *hits* **Flemish** *over the head with his newspaper and walks off.*

Derek   Happens every time, bloody spies!

He exits.

Blonde   For God's sake, Flemish, stand down. I'll be there shortly.

Flemish   Sorry, Blonde.

Himmel   Excuse me, did I hear that you needed a light?

Flemish *turns and sees* **Himmel** *still sitting on the bench's other side.*

Flemish   Oh, that, no thanks. I don't even smoke, terrible habit. (*Pause.*) Wait! Yes! That's it! Stand down the troops, Blonde. I've got everything under control. I'd love a light, thank you.

Himmel   What brand of cigarettes are you smoking?

Flemish   Ah, well . . . wait, blast! I can't find them. Hold that thought – don't move a muscle. I must have dropped them in the scuffle. Hang on, won't be a minute.

Flemish *looks for the cigarettes.* **Mr Hugs** *enters.* **Mr Hugs** *taps* **Himmel**, *and he tries to run.* **Mr Hugs** *grabs him.*

Himmel   Help!

Flemish   No need to help, you just relax!

Hugs *kills* **Himmel** *and places him back on the bench.*

Flemish   Got them! Right where were we? Ah, yes, do you smoke this brand?

Himmel *doesn't react.*

Flemish   What's the next line? Blonde? Blonde?! Roger?

Derek (*off*)   It's Derek!

Flemish   Think, Flemish! Think!

A moment, then –

Oh! One day, I promise I'll take you to Lancaster.

Himmel *drops into* **Flemish**'s *arms.*

Flemish   It worked!

Blonde *runs in.*

Flemish   Did you see that, Blonde? It worked!

He picks up the suitcase, still gripped in **Himmel**'s *hand.*

Blonde   He's dead.

Flemish   Are you sure? He might just be a sleeper agent.

He moves his arm. It is stiff.

Flemish   Roger mortis.

Derek   It's rigor!

Flemish   I thought it was Derek?

Derek   Oh, bugger off!

Blonde   No pulse.

Flemish   Oh my God. I'm a murderer.

Blonde   It wasn't you, Flemish. (*To* **Writer**.) Let go of the case . . .

Flemish   Oh, thank God.

Blonde   But he's still dead. Looks like he suffocated.

Flemish   Oh, well. The important thing is that we all learnt a valuable lesson; smoking is bad for you.

Blonde   Now we have no idea where to find Herr Ring and no hope of getting your manuscript back.

Flemish   What are we going to do, Blonde? I'm not sure I'm cut out for all this. Usually in my books, when a mission fails, I just write in a convenient solution. Something miraculous or unexpected will suddenly appear and advance the plot. But this is real life, we're doomed!

Blonde *searches* **Himmel**'s *pockets and pulls out a slip of paper.*

Flemish   What's that?

Blonde   A one-way train ticket to Monte Carlo.

Flemish   Well, that was convenient!

INT. A TRAIN TO MONTE CARLO – DAY.

A train crosses the stage. **Flemish** *and* **Blonde** *are seated, the scenery rolling past.* **Flemish** *is trying to open the suitcase. The* **Producer**, *as* **Barman**, *enters.*

Flemish   Wow! A train to Monte Carlo!

Barman   What would you like to drink, sir?

Writer (*to* **Producer**)   You're French.

Barman (*in an accent*)   What would you like to drink, sir?

Flemish   I'll have a vodka martini shaken, not stirred.

Blonde   A real spy would never order such a ridiculous drink.

Barman   And for you, madam?

Blonde   I'll have a single gin, double vodka, triple whiskey and quadruple rum shaken, stirred and jiggled.

Barman   Mange tout!

The **Barman** *exits. The suitcase pops open.*

Flemish   Look, Blonde, a teddy bear!

Blonde   That's not a teddy bear. It's a calling card. Mr Hugs is on this train.

Mr Hugs *music spike.*

Flemish   Mr Hugs? He sounds nice.

Blonde   Don't be fooled by the name. He's a remorseless killer with a deadly cuddle.

Flemish   How can you be sure it's him?

Blonde   Because he was an old friend, an agent working for MI6 like me.

Producer   Flashback!

The lights change. Over the following, we see **Mr** *and* **Mrs Hugs** *silhouettes in a flashback.*

Blonde   Mr Hugs was a double agent working with the Russians. While undercover in Moscow, he fell in love with his contact, Romanov Kaplinka. When his mission ended, he

refused to leave her behind, knowing she'd be killed. They
fled together, married in secret, and were placed in
government protection. I was at the wedding – the whole
family was there, there were hugs, hugs all around. But
during their honeymoon, Hugs was ambushed while out
buying champagne, chocolates and a teddy bear. Mrs Hugs
vanished, presumed dead. Mr Hugs was taken, tortured and
broken. Now, he's a weapon for hire – an emotionless
assassin. The agent I knew is long gone. All that remains is
. . .

Mr Hugs   Hugs!

The lights change back to the train.

Blonde   And his signature calling card . . .

Flemish   A teddy bear. What do we do?

Blonde   We need to find Mr Hugs and retrieve your
manuscript. Let's check the other carriages and keep your
eyes open for anything suspicious.

They open the first carriage door, revealing a murder. The
Murderer *freezes.*

Murderer   Morning!

Murder Victim   Ugh.

Blonde   These long train journeys can be a real killer. Let's
keep looking.

They open another carriage door to reveal a kidnapping. The
Kidnapper *freezes.*

Kidnapper   Morning.

Kidnap Victim (*muffled*)   Morning!

Blonde   This must be the quiet carriage. Try the last one.

*They open a final carriage door to reveal a couple having
afternoon tea.*

Woman   Morning.

Man (*eating a scone*)   Hugs.

Blonde *closes the doors again.*

Blonde   Damn. He's gone.

Flemish   Wait a minute.

Blonde   What?

Flemish   The man's scone. The jam was underneath the cream. What train is this?

Blonde   The Devonshire Express to Monte Carlo.

Flemish   The Devonshire Express would never serve their scones the Cornish way!

Blonde   It was Mr Hugs!

She opens the doors, but **Mr Hugs** *is gone.*

Flemish   He's gone!

Blonde   The window!

Blonde *and* **Flemish** *run to open the window, the wind rushing in. They spin, and the perspective shifts to –*

EXT. A TRAIN – DAY.

Flemish *is looking out of the window, the wind buffeting him.*

Flemish   There he is! He's getting away!

Blonde   After him! Climb out of the window!

Flemish   Are you mad?

Blonde   Do you want your manuscript or not?

With difficulty, **Flemish** *climbs out of the window.*

Flemish   Good luck, Blonde. Let me know if you need a hand, it's quite difficult –

Blonde *follows easily.*

Flemish   There he is!

Blonde   Shuffle along the side of the train!

They shuffle along the side of the train.

Flemish   He's climbed up onto the roof!

Blonde   We'll have to climb up after him.

Flemish   Blonde, give me a hand!

They climb onto the roof. As they do, a massive puff of steam floods the stage and the lights grow bright. When they return, the perspective has shifted to –

EXT. A TRAIN ROOF – DAY.

Flemish *and* **Blonde** *are on the roof of the train.*

Flemish   I can't tell which way is up!

Blonde   It's all a matter of perspective. Walk this way!

They walk along the roof of the train.

Blonde   Careful, Flemish. Stay low and keep an eye out for tun –

Flemish   Tunnel!

They duck. The lights dip.

Flemish   Sorry, Blonde, what were you saying?

Blonde   I was saying, stay low and keep an eye out for tun –

Flemish   Tunnel!

They duck. The lights dip. When the lights come back up, **Mr Hugs** *has appeared.*

Flemish   It's Mr Hugs! Sorry, Blonde, what were you saying?

Blonde   I was saying, stay low and keep an eye out for tun –

Producer   Slo-mo!

Flemish *turns to see the tunnel racing towards him.*

Flemish   Tunnel!

At the last second, **Blonde** *pulls* **Flemish** *to the floor. The lights dip, slower this time, and, when they come back up,* **Mr Hugs** *has vanished.*

Flemish   He's gone!

Blonde   Get behind me, Flemish. He still has the manuscript. Where is he?

They swap positions. **Mr Hugs** *appears on the other side, nearing* **Flemish.**

Flemish   Blonde!

Blonde   Wait a minute!

Flemish   Blonde!

Blonde   Quiet! I'm looking for Mr Hugs.

Flemish *hesitates, then –*

Flemish   Blonde!

Hugs   Hugs?

Flemish *throws* **Mr Hugs** *the teddy, and* **Mr Hugs** *drops the manuscript.*

Flemish   I've got the manuscript!

Blonde *punches* **Mr Hugs.**

Blonde   Look! A passing cable car! Jump!

A cable car appears. **Blonde** *and* **Flemish** *jump. Blackout.*

INT. CABLE CAR – NIGHT.

In the darkness, we hear –

Flemish   We did it! We've got the manuscript! Oh, that's nice. What a lovely celebratory hug! But, Blonde, do you have to hug me quite so tightly?

Blonde   I'm not hugging you.

Flemish   If you're not, it must be . . . Oh my God.

Hugs   Hugs!

Flemish   I think I left my oven on!

Blonde   It's Mr Hugs!

SMASH! In flashing vignettes, **Blonde** *and* **Mr Hugs** *battle in the cable car.*

Flemish   Damn! He's got the manuscript. Give that back!

A ripping is heard.

Damn! I've torn it!

Blonde   A passing train! Jump!

INT. A TRAIN TO MONTE CARLO – DAY.

Lights up. They are back on the train. They are remarkably dishevelled.

Blonde   I knew we shouldn't have trusted National Rail.

Flemish   At least we have the final page of my manuscript.

Blonde *gestures to the folder.* **Flemish** *opens it to reveal a single page.*

A ticking sound is heard.

Flemish   I thought your watch didn't tell the time?

Blonde   It doesn't. The bear!

Flemish   I know. It's cute, isn't it? I love a teddy bear.

Blonde   That's not a teddy bear, it's a teddy bomb!

Ticket Inspector (*off*)   Tickets, please!

Flemish   What are we going to do? There's a bomb on this train – and I haven't got a ticket!

Blonde   You need to start thinking like a spy.

Flemish   I'm a writer!

Blonde   What would Dick Hardwood do?

Ticket Inspector (*off*)   Tickets, please!

The **Producer**, *as* **Ticket Inspector**, *appears.*

Ticket Inspector   Tickets, please!

Flemish *punches the* **Ticket Inspector**.

Ticket Inspector   Thank you! And your railcard?

Flemish *hands the* **Ticket Inspector** *the teddy bomb.*

Ticket Inspector   Thank you. Next stop, Monte Carlo!

The **Ticket Inspector** *exits. For a moment, the beeping gets louder, then – BANG! A party popper goes off from stage right.*

A moment.

The **Barman**'*s charred hand appears with a drink.*

Barman   Your drink, madam . . .

Blonde *takes it.*

Blonde   No wonder they go on strike.

INT. MONTE CARLO – DAY.

Monte Carlo casino. **Flemish** *and* **Blonde** *enter. The* **Writer** *and* **Producer** *enter as* **Herr Ring** *and* **Croupier**.

Flemish   Wow, Monte Carlo!

Blonde   Now, keep an eye out. Herr Ring could be anywhere. Nobody knows his super-secret evil identity because of an ingenious disguise, so everyone is a suspect.

Croupier   Blackjack! And the winner is Herr Ring.

Blonde   Herr Ring.

Flemish   No thanks, I've still got my walnut cake.

Blonde   Join that table, and remember –

Flemish   Just do precisely what you say.

He sits at the table.

I'll put the whole lot on red . . . No, you idiot!

Croupier   This is blackjack, sir.

Herr Ring   Hit me.

The **Croupier** *deals him a card.*

Herr Ring   Hit me.

The **Croupier** *deals him another.*

Flemish   Hit me.

The **Croupier** *hits him.*

Flemish   Thank you. Now deal me in.

The **Croupier** *deals him in.*

Croupier   Blackjack! And the winner is –

Flemish   The name's Blonde, Jane –

Herr Ring   Jane Blonde.

He turns. **Blonde** *is there.*

Blonde   Herr Ring.

Flemish   Herr Ring.

Blonde   No, you don't have to repeat that.

Flemish   No, you don't have to repeat that.

Blonde   Good to –

Flemish   Good to –

Blonde   Hit me.

Flemish   Hit me.

The **Croupier** *hits him.*

Blonde   Thank you.

Blonde *tips the* **Croupier***, he then exits.*

Blonde   Good to see you, old friend.

Herr Ring   I wish I could say the same.

Blonde   Why don't you remove those incredibly dark sunglasses?

Herr Ring   Remove my ingenious disguise and reveal my super-secret evil identity? Never!

Blonde   You've lost weight.

Herr Ring   Let's just say I've been on a killer diet. Ha! Because I kill people.

Blonde   Fancy a game while we're here?

Herr Ring   I'm afraid you have nothing to tempt me.

Blonde   What about the final instalment of the Dick Hardwood series?

Herr Ring   You mean . . . Zis?!

He snaps his fingers and **Mr Hugs** *emerges with the manuscript.*

Hugs   Hugs!

Herr Ring *gestures to the manuscript – in the wrong direction.*

A beat.

They correct themselves, finishing on the wrong side of each other again.

A beat.

They correct themselves. Wrong again.

The **Producer** *gives up and hands* **Herr Ring** *the manuscript.*

Hugs   Hugs.

Hugs *exits.*

Herr Ring   As you can see, I already have the manuscript right here!

Blonde   Yes, but that manuscript is useless without this –

She clicks her fingers, and **Flemish** *reveals . . . the cake.*

Flemish   A walnut cake.

Herr Ring   Get that away from me, you idiot!

Blonde   The final page.

He puts it back and reveals . . . the final page.

Blonde   Do we have a deal?

She puts out her hand. **Herr Ring** *does the same.* **Blonde** *moves to shake it.*

Herr Ring   What's the game? Blackjacks?

Blonde   Not with your dodgy cards.

Herr Ring   Crabs?

Blonde   Rigged dice, I don't think so.

Herr Ring   Roulette?

Blonde   You haven't got the balls.

Herr Ring   Then what?

Blonde   An ancient game of nerves, skill and little wooden blocks.

The **Croupier** *appears with a Jenga tower. He positions himself carefully between* **Blonde** *and* **Herr Ring**. **Herr Ring** *makes the first move, toppling the Jenga tower.*

Croupier   Jenga! And the winner is Blonde!

Herr Ring   You played well.

Blonde Call it beginner's luck. Now, hand over the manuscript.

Herr Ring Of course. But first, what do you think of Mr Hugs's new glasses?

Mr Hugs *appears in his new, incredibly dark glasses. He reveals a flash-bang.*

Blonde Shield your eyes, Flemish! He's got a flash-bang!

He throws it to the floor. BANG!

Flemish Ah! I can't see a thing!

Herr Ring Run, Hugs!

Blonde Quickly, after the manuscript!

Herr Ring Ha! It's already on its way to the top-secret location of EVIW HQ.

Blonde I've got him!

Flemish I've got him!

Blonde I've got him!

Flemish (*vamp*) No, I've – open your eyes . . .

The **Actress** *opens her eyes and realises she is not holding* **Herr Ring** *but someone else. She lets go quickly and apologises.*

Blonde Tell me the location of EVIW HQ.

Herr Ring Over my dead body. Speaking of which, where's that walnut cake?

Flemish Here! Why?

He reveals the cake, and **Herr Ring** *eats it in one.*

Blonde No! He's allergic to walnuts! You'll rot in hell for this!

Herr Ring See you . . . there. Ha! Because I can't see wiz ze glasses!

He drops. Throughout the following, **Herr Ring** *dies very slowly.*

Flemish   Nuts.

Blonde   Quickly, call an ambulance!

Herr Ring   *Nein, nein, nein!*

Croupier   Don't worry, I know the number.

The **Croupier** *runs in with a rotary telephone. He dials. Slowly. We wait.*

Croupier   Hello! I need an ambulance. (*Pause.*) Oh, sorry. Wrong number. (*Dials again.*) Hello! I need an ambulance. It's an emergency. A pulse, I'll check. (*He hangs up. Goes to* **Herr Ring**. *Goes back to the phone. Dials.*) Hello! I just called. Oh, I'm sorry, I must have been speaking to one of your colleagues. (*Pause.*) He's just transferring me.

Blonde   This is exactly why I didn't want you to come on this mission.

Flemish   I was just trying to help.

Blonde   Well, don't.

Croupier   Yes, me again. Good news: he has a pulse!

Blonde   Without the location of EVIW, we may never retrieve the manuscript.

Croupier   His address? It's 'Mr Lovely's Lovely Wellness Resort, AKA the secret location of EVIW HQ, third furthest island from Maui'.

Flemish   Well, that was convenient!

Croupier   But come quickly! He's dying!

Herr Ring *finally dies.*

Croupier   Wait, don't worry. He's dead!

Blonde   I hope you brought your passport.

They exit. After a moment, the phone begins to ring. The **Croupier** *re-enters. As he is about to answer, the* **Stuntman** *appears.*

Stuntman   Albert, someone is asking for you –

Producer   Get off stage!

Stuntman   It sounded important! Something about Jeff?

Producer   Do not engage!

Finally, the **Producer***, as* **Croupier***, picks up the phone.*

Croupier   Hello. Yes, Mr Lovely. They're on the way . . .

Blackout.

INT. AEROPLANE – NIGHT.

An aeroplane. **Flemish** *and* **Blonde** *are in their seats.*

Voiceover   Welcome aboard the flight to Mr Lovely Lovely's Wellness Retreat, AKA the top-secret location of EVIW HQ, third furthest island from Maui.

Flemish   Ah, air travel! The safest mode of transport in the world. I think I'm going to get some shut-eye!

An air **Steward** *appears. He is asking people for their food order.*

Steward   Chicken or beef, sir? Chicken or beef, madam?

The **Steward** *approaches* **Flemish***. He is asleep.*

Steward   Shhh.

If the audience are making noise/laughing, the **Steward***, if played by the producer can vamp with them in an attempt to get them to be quiet.*

The **Steward** *turns to* **Blonde***.*

Steward   And for you, madam? Chicken or . . . DEATH!

The **Steward** *pulls a knife on* **Blonde***, and she grabs his arm. A series of fighting vignettes intercut with the model rocking follows.*

Eventually, a doll falls from the model plane, and **Blonde** *sits calmly again.*

Blonde   Now I see why nobody likes plane food.

Flemish (*taking off his mask*)   Did I miss something?

Blonde   Oh, nothing. Just a spot of turbulence.

INT. MR LOVELY'S LOVELY WELLNESS RETREAT – DAY.

The **Producer** *as* **Jubbly** *enters. He stands on one leg, in tree pose, for a long time. Eventually,* **Flemish** *enters.*

Jubbly   Mr Flemish, welcome to Mr Lovely's Lovely Wellness Retreat! How was your flight?

Flemish   Oh. It was excellent, thank you! That's why I always fly Michael Mullaney's!

The Michael Mullaney's Used Plane Dealership jingle plays.

Jubbly   And who is your guest?

Blonde   The name's –

Flemish   Blonde –

Jubbly   Jane Blonde. Your reputation precedes you, Blonde.

Blonde   I didn't catch your name.

Jubbly   My name is Mr Jubbly. I look after the resort here for Mr Lovely.

Blonde   I see. I would very much like to meet this Lovely, Jubbly.

Jubbly   Hmm, this lovely jubbly what?

Actor   What?

Producer   What?

Stuntman   What?

Beat.

Blonde   Mr Lovely. When can I meet him?

Jubbly   All in good time. First, allow me to show you the resort. Come, we will take the helicopter.

A model helicopter appears. **Jubbly** *is at the controls. He flies it precariously over and around the audience.*

Jubbly   In total, there are over one million hectares of land.

Blonde   How quaint.

Jubbly   Mr Lovely has investments in many philanthropic fields, including education, scientific research, affordable housing, healthcare, agriculture and, of course, a little sideline in manufacturing weapons of mass destruction.

Flemish   What?

Jubbly   Only joking!

Blonde   Next, you'll tell me he has a space station.

Jubbly   That would be Lovely –

Writer   No space!

Producer (*ad libbing as* **Jubbly**)   However, Mr Lovely lacked artistic ambition.

The helicopter drops out of the air.

Flemish   What a smooth landing.

Jubbly   This is Mr Lovely's country estate.

Flemish   Lovely.

Jubbly   Yes. That is his name. Complete with coy carp pond, piranha-infested jacuzzi and the Great Pyramid of Giza. Mr Lovely had it brought from Egypt block by block.

They look. Up and up and up.

Flemish   What a knob!

Jubbly   Indeed. Mr Lovely has the biggest collection of doorknobs in the world.

Blonde   What's that suspicious-looking clifftop facility over there?

Jubbly   Suspicious-looking clifftop facility? I'm not sure what you're talking about.

Blonde   The one behind you.

The clifftop facility is revealed in the distance.

Jubbly   Oh, that? Why, it's nothing. Just a perfectly innocent but suspicious-looking clifftop facility. We mainly use it to store suspicious-looking crates when we don't have room in the house. What did you think it was, some sort of secret laboratory?

He laughs. **Flemish** *joins in.*

Blonde   Yes.

They stop.

Jubbly   Well, it's not. The whole area is strictly out of bounds. Please wait here whilst I fetch Mr Lovely.

He exits.

Flemish   Nice man. I think you might be right, though. There's something suspicious about that suspicious-looking facility.

Blonde   I'll take a photo and return it to HQ for analysis.

Flemish   I didn't know you had a camera.

Blonde   You wouldn't. It's a spy camera.

She takes a small box resembling a mini-camera from her breast pocket.

Blonde   Mint?

Flemish   No, thank you.

Blonde *puts the mints away, then reveals a huge camera.*

She takes a photo with a big flash, then puts it away.

Flemish   Amazing. If only we could send it with some sort of electronic mail.

Jubbly *re-enters.*

Jubbly   What was that?

Flemish   Nothing.

Blonde   Mint?

Jubbly   No, thank you. Mr Lovely is ready for you now. He's just finishing up on the eighteenth tee of the Old Course at St Andrews.

Flemish   The real thing?

The **Writer** *is* **Lovely** *with a golf club.*

Lovely   Yes, Mr Flemish. The one in Scotland is a replica.

They reveal the miniature golf hole.

Flemish   Impressive.

Lovely   Mr Flemish, I am a huge fan. And who is your friend?

Blonde   My name is –

Flemish   Blonde.

Jubbly   Jane Blonde.

Actress   Right, will I ever get to say my own name in this thing or –

Lovely   Ah, yes, the pleasure is all mine. Do you play Blonde?

Blonde   I've dabbled. But I didn't bring my clubs.

Lovely   Please, use mine. I insist.

Blonde   Lovely, lovely. Four!

She takes the club and sinks the ball in one (or more) attempts.

Lovely   A hole-in-one. Well played. But I take it you didn't come here for golf.

Blonde   We're looking for a stolen manuscript.

Lovely   Oh dear, not one of Mr Flemish's? I'm such a big fan. If you find Mr Flemish's manuscript, let me know. I'd kill to read it.

Blonde   I don't doubt it.

Lovely   And you must join us for dinner. Mr Jubbly is making his famous potato soup. That is, if you're not tied up.

Blonde   I'm sure I won't be.

Lovely   Good. I just hope you're not bound to any other commitments.

Blonde   Don't worry, I'm not.

Lovely   Good. I just mean, I hope you're not roped into anything else.

Flemish   I'm beginning to feel like he's trying to say something.

Lovely   No! Not at all!

They laugh. **Jubbly** *takes it too far.*

Lovely   Anyway, I must dash! Come Jubbly; we need to finish skinning the prisoners.

Jubbly *corrects her under his breath.*

Lovely   I mean . . . potatoes. That we have shackled –

Jubbly *corrects her under his breath.*

Lovely   I mean . . . soaking. In the dungeon –

Jubbly *corrects her under his breath.*

Lovely   I mean . . . in the kitchen.

Jubbly   Yes, sir. Then, we'll skin the prisoners we have shackled in the dungeon.

Lovely *and* **Jubbly** *go to leave.*

Blonde   Mr Lovely, don't forget your club.

Lovely   Give it to Jubbly. He's very good with his hands.

Mr Jubbly *takes the club and tries to bend it out of shape, struggling. He gives it to the* **Stagehand** *to try. They fail.*

Producer   You're fired! . . . Help me, Gary.

He takes the club back and exits, intimidatingly.

Flemish   He's a bit of a sore loser, isn't he! Fancy a spot of lymphatic drainage, Blonde?

Blonde   You can, Flemish. I have work to do for Queen and country.

Flemish   Don't you mean King?

Blonde   They've been trying to get funding for this film since 2012.

The **Producer** *pops his head through the curtain.*

Producer   And remember, Gary, shares are still available! Buy one – get the rest free! Now strap in its time for the cliffhanger!

CLIFFHANGER! (PART ONE)

The following is one continuous scene that is intercut, like a film. We switch between **Blonde** *at the base of the cliff talking to* **MMM** *in MI6 HQ and* **Flemish** *and* **Mr Jubbly** *in one of the resort's treatment rooms. During the scene the actors switch between locations.*

EXT. CLIFF / MI6 HQ – DUSK.

Blonde *is at the bottom of the cliff talking to* **MMM** *at MI6 HQ (split-screen).*

Blonde   Sir, can you hear me?

MMM   Loud and clear, Blonde.

Blonde   I've tracked the manuscript to Mr Lovely's Lovely Wellness Resort.

MMM   Lovely.

Blonde   Yes that is his name. Mr Lovely Wellness Resort is a front for EVIW HQ.

Producer (*jumping in*)   Cliffhanger!

Writer (*shoving him off*)   No!

Blonde   Sir?

MMM   Interesting I've just remembered something from Flemish's file. When he had his accident, he recovered at Mr Lovely's Lovely Wellness Resort!

Producer (*jumping in*)   Cliffhanger!

Writer (*shoving him off*)   No!

Blonde   That's odd. He didn't mention it to me.

MMM   Well, apparently . . . he has no memory of it.

INT. TREATMENT ROOM – DUSK.

Jubbly *is preparing* **Flemish** *for a treatment.*

Jubbly   Ah Mr Flemish how was your lymphatic drainage?

Flemish   I feel fresh as a daisy.

Jubbly   This subsequent treatment is even more relaxing. Pop yourself up here and we'll get started.

Flemish   And you're sure it's safe?

Jubbly   Perfectly safe! In fact I think you'll find the whole process very . . . hypnotic.

Flemish   And the straps?

Jubbly   They're for your own safety Mr Flemish, just try to relax.

Jubbly *straps* **Flemish** *into the brainwashing machine.*

EXT. CLIFF / MI6 HQ – DUSK.

Blonde   Did you receive my photographs of the suspicious looking clifftop facility?

MMM   Yes we've had our best and most diverse white male minds analyse them and they've reached a startling conclusion.

Blonde   Which is?

MMM   It's definitely suspicious.

MMM   Any idea what it is?

Blonde   Not yet, sir, but I'm on my way up there now.

MMM   Be careful, Blonde; if you fall, it would mean almost certain death!

Producer (*jumping in*)   Cliffhanger!

Writer   No!

She shoves him off.

INT. TREATMENT ROOM – DUSK.

Jubbly   Can I get you anything, tea? Coffee? Perhaps a nice ripe watermelon?

Flemish   No, thank you.

Jubbly   Very well let's begin. Now you may feel a slight vibration.

Flemish *vibrates wildly.*

Flemish   I can barely feel a thing.

Jubbly   You may also feel a strong desire to scream out in pain as we attempt to break your mind.

Flemish   That's nice.

Jubbly   Oh yes, just try to relax.

EXT. CLIFF / MI6 HQ – DUSK.

Blonde *throws a line to the top of the cliff.*

Blonde   Sir, I'm getting ready to start my ascent. Rope secu–

She braces the rope, and it splits in half.

MMM   Sorry, Blonde. You cut out. It's a pretty bad line.

Blonde   You're telling me.

Producer (*off*)   Use the safety rope!

*The **Actress** reveals the safety rope and finishes preparing.*

Blonde   Rope secure; I am about to make my assent. But first, a quick drink on the rocks. Behind this rock.

Blonde *steps behind a rock.*

INT. TREATMENT ROOM – DUSK.

*The chair is still rocking violently. The **Producer** is struggling to stop it and free the **Stuntman**.*

Jubbly   Well, Mr Flemish, phase one of the treatment is now complete. I'll just undo these straps and you can relax in the waiting room whilst I prepare for the final phase.

Stuntman (*under his breath*)   I'm stuck!

Jubbly   Yes, feel free to stretch your legs in the gardens if you prefer. The peacocks are delightful at this time of year.

*The **Producer** continues to struggle to free him.*

Flemish   I'll see you soon.

Jubbly   See you soon!

EXT. CLIFF / MI6 HQ – DUSK.

MMM   Ah, Blonde, you're back. (*Beat.*) Blonde? (*Beat.*) Have you finished your drink yet, Blonde? (*Covering.*) Must be having a double! (*Beat.*) . . . a double! (*Beat.*) Maybe I could have a stunt double as well.

Producer (*off*)   She means you, you're the stunt double. It's your cue!

Stuntman (*off*)   Why did you do the straps so tight?

INT. TREATMENT ROOM – DUSK.

The **Producer** *and* **Stuntman** *are still wrestling to stop the machine and free him, when, unbeknownst to them, the lights come up.*

Producer   This was never a problem for Jeff.

Stuntman   Oh bloody Jeff!

They realise they've been caught and freeze.

EXT. CLIFF / MI6 HQ – DUSK.

MMM   Blonde, are you there?

Actress (*poking out*)   Are you talking to me?

MMM   Yes, Blonde, you need to start climbing now.

Actress   I'm not doing it. He's the stuntman!

INT. TREATMENT ROOM – DUSK.

The **Producer** *is now straddling the* **Stuntman***, who is still rocking uncontrollably.*

Producer   Just making some very minor and definitely scripted adjustments!

EXT. CLIFF / MI6 HQ – DUSK.

Light back up, just as the **Writer** *pulls the* **Actress** *onstage.*

MMM   There you are, Blonde! Now tell me all the information you have urgently –

Producer (*off*)   Stall, stall!

MMM   But we've all the time in the world, so don't you dare make it snappy!

The **Stuntman** *bursts into the scene dressed as* **Blonde**.

Stuntman   I'm here, don't worry!

He notices the **Actress**.

Stuntman   It's me – your identical twin, Jane . . . Blonder.

The **Stuntman** *shoves the* **Actress** *off, into –*

INT. TREATMENT ROOM – DUSK.

Light up as the **Actress** *appears with the* **Producer** *in the other scene.*

Jubbly   You're back . . . Mr Flemish. Feeling invigorated?

Actress   No!

Jubbly   Good.

Actress   I'm contracted for one role in this play.

Producer   Film!

Actress   No.

Producer   I'll give you a tenner.

Actress   Fifty.

Producer   Sixty.

Actress   Deal.

EXT. CLIFF / MI6 HQ – DUSK.

The **Stuntman** *(as* **Blonde***) is attached to the safety rope and climbing the ladder, approaching the summit.*

MMM   Blonde, come in!

Stuntman   Sir! I'm nearly at the top.

MMM   Very good, Blonde, but be careful – we're forecasting a little rain –

The **Producer** *squirts a small water pistol, but it is pathetic. He reveals a huge one and fires a massive jet at the* **Stuntman**.

MMM *(improvising)*   A lot of rain! And minor winds –

The **Producer** *creates wind around the ladder, knocking the* **Stuntman**.

MMM   A hurricane!

Stuntman   Don't worry, sir, I'm safely attached.

The second rope snaps. The **Stuntman** *loses his footing but holds on.*

Stuntman   Could somebody pass me the safety rope?

Writer   That is the safety rope.

Stuntman   Wait, what?

INT. TREATMENT ROOM – DUSK.

Actress *is now strapped into the chair with a bag on her head.*

Jubbly   Now, Mr Flemish, you should start feeling very agreeable.

Actress   As soon as this is over, I'll go straight to my union rep!

Jubbly   Yes, that's right; Watermelon can be very pleasant after a massage.

Actress   I will shove that Watermelon straight up your –

As the thunder strikes, the ladder falls through the curtain with a clatter.

Stuntman (*off*)   Ah!

EXT. CLIFF / MI6 HQ – DUSK.

The ladder has fallen but the **Stuntman** *is holding on, dangling.*

Stuntman   I'm alright! (*He looks down.*) I'm not alright!

MMM   Just hang in there, Blonde! (*As* **Writer**.) It's nearly the cue for Randy Lust to come on and pull you up.

Stuntman   But I play Randy Lust!

Ding! Ding! Ding! A phone goes off.

Producer   Right, whose phone is that? This is the theatre! Who was it?

Stuntman   Sorry. It must be my aunty. I'll just –

The **Stuntman** *reaches for his pocket.*

Producer   No!

Writer   Don't let go!

Actress (*still bound and covered*)   What's going on?

The **Producer** *grabs the* **Stuntman** *by the legs and holds him.*

Producer   Oops! Just me! Can you get that?

The **Writer** *gets his phone and turns away.*

Stuntman   Is it my aunty?

Actress   Can somebody take this bag off my head and tell me what the hell is happening?

The **Writer** *turns back around.*

Writer   It's Jeff. He's sending bailiff to repossess the set and collect what he is owed.

Producer *lets go of* **Stuntman**.

Producer   They're shutting us down?

Stuntman   I'm going to die!

Producer   Now that's a cliffhanger!

Blackout.

Interval

During the interval, the cast in character attempt to tidy up the set.

The **Producer** *conscripts the* **Stagehand***, or someone in the audience, to clear up the Jenga.*

The **Stuntman** *attempts to bring on a ladder and remove the movie sign, he fails and the* **Actress** *does it for him.*

The **Producer** *tries to buy an ice cream and the* **Writer** *stops him.*

etc.

Act Two

DICK HARDWOOD

The following is a scene from a Dick Hardwood novel and should feel tonally different from the rest of the piece. An alarm sounds. **Dick Hardwood** *and* **Cecilia Romping** *are defusing a bomb.*

Narrator *(V/O)*   It was the kind of night that stank of trouble. Somewhere, time was ticking – and so was a bomb.

Dick   Quickly, Cecilia, you need to disarm that bomb, whilst I hold off the guards.

Narrator   Dick Hardwood was a man who chewed bullets for breakfast and stared death in the face and told it to shave.

Cecilia Romping   Oh, Dick, what do I do?

Narrator   Cecilia Romping – half lipstick, half dynamite, next to that bomb, she was smoking.

Dick   Celia, don't smoke next to that bomb! What can you see?

Cecilia   I see some red tubes, flashing lights, a bunch of wires . . . and everything is connected to a watch?

Dick   What type of watch?

Cecilia   A Rolex Tudor.

Narrator   A Rolex Tudor. Classy. Expensive. The kind of timepiece that tells more than the time – it tells secrets. Dick owned forty-seven of them.

Dick   I know how to defuse that bomb. All you need to do is find the blue wire.

SFX: The power dies. The stage goes black. The bomb ticks louder.

Cecilia   Oh, Dick, I can't see a thing!

Dick   They've cut the power. Here – night vision goggles.

Cecilia   Do you always carry these?

Dick   Of course. After all, half the day is night.

Cecilia *puts on the goggles. The stage glows an eerie green.*

Cecilia   It worked. I can see all the cables!

Dick   Well, what are you waiting for? Cut the blue one!

Cecilia   Which one is blue? They're all green now!

Dick   Here, use my torch!

He turns on the torch. A blinding flash.

Cecilia   Ah! I'm blind!

Dick *rips off the goggles.*

Cecilia   I can see again. It's a miracle!

Narrator   She saw light, life . . . and certain death, blinking red at two beats a second.

SFX: The beeping speeds up.

Dick   Good, now cut the wire, quickly!

Cecilia   I still can't see it!

Dick   What now?

Cecilia   I'm colour blind!

Narrator   Of course. In a world of smoke and mirrors, even the colours lied.

Dick   Okay, when in doubt I always use my right hand.

Cecilia   Are you sure, Dick?

Narrator   She didn't trust men. She didn't trust bombs. But she trusted Dick Hardwood's right hand – and that was her most dangerous gamble yet.

Dick   Yes.

Narrator   She hesitated.

Dick   Do it.

Narrator   She hesitated again.

Dick   Now!

Narrator   She finally did it.

Cecilia   I did it, Dick!

Narrator   The world couldn't end. Not tonight. Not on Hardwood's watch. Not while he still had a fist, a torch and a woman –

A telephone rings.

INT. MI6 HQ – DAY.

Lights up on **MMM** *sitting at his desk, reading the book.*

MMM   Damn, just as it was getting good! (*Picking up.*) MI6 headquarters, this is MMM. Go on . . . Yes . . . Interesting . . . Mmm. No, I wasn't saying my name. That would be MMM, not mmm. Look, get to the point, would you? This is the emergency line! Yes, I would like to reschedule my moustache pruning to Thursday. See you then.

He puts the phone down.

Frowning *enters carrying a chess set.*

MMM   Ah, Frowning.

Frowning   Hello, MMM, it's good to see you.

MMM   Tell your face. Have you read much of this Dick Hardwood rubbish?

Frowning   Can't say that I have, sir.

MMM   It's absolute trash, I love it. Right, Frowning, let's make this quick, I've got company on the way. Knight to F14, check!

Frowning   We're not playing chess, sir. I'm here to talk about the rotten apple.

MMM   Yes squishy little bugger. Picked it up from the staff canteen. Now, come on, make your move.

Frowning   I am trying to use chess pieces to represent the potential double agents.

MMM   Excellent visual metaphor! Now, it's your move. Wait. Sorry. No. It's mine.

Frowning   Sir!

MMM   Sorry! Go on.

Frowning *picks up a chess piece and holds it in the air. As he picks up each piece, a large close-up of the piece is also shown. Each piece has a different photo of the* **Producer** *on it.*

Frowning   Agent Sheringham, Code name Tinker.

He holds up the next piece.

Agent Archibald, Code name Tailor.

MMM   Is he any good? I might need my trousers done after that big lunch.

Frowning   Code names, sir.

MMM   Ah, yes. Exciting!

Frowning *holds up the next piece.*

Frowning   Byron, soldier.

MMM   Brave chap.

Frowning *places the pieces.*

Frowning   Now we drop Sailor because it's too close to Tailor; we also drop Rich Man, Poor Man and Beggar Man because they are too close to a famous film, and we don't want to be sued. So, we move on to another nursery rhyme. Bletchley, Humpty, Springfield, Dumpty. Franklin, Incy. Jocelyn, Wincey. Shelly, Muffet. Arkwright, Mo.

MMM   Mo?

Frowning   That's right, Mo, which makes Angelo, Jennings, Powell, Enie, Meenie and Minnie. With me so far?

MMM   This is the strangest game of chess I've ever played.

Frowning   Herbert is Jack, and Deeds is Sprat. Mary is quite contrary, and Natkin is Cole. Finally, we have Hutchins and Hickory, and that leaves Lust.

MMM   Dickory?

Frowning   No, Doc.

MMM   I'm flattered, but I'm not a doctor.

Frowning   Lust is Doc, sir.

MMM   Randy Lust, secret double agent? I never would've guessed. Damn, so it could be any one of these people. They are all so different, it will be hard to narrow it down.

Frowning   I'll do my best, sir.

He goes to exit.

MMM   Good man! Oh, and Frowning, give us a smile once in a while. You're a spy for Christ's sake!

Frowning *tries to smile and then leaves.*

The phone rings. **MMM** *picks it up.*

MMM   MI6 headquarters. Mr Cashless Payment, finally! You know, we really need to change the ringtone of the emergency line. Well, what is it? (*Pause.*) Yes. (*Pause.*) Go on. (*Pause.*) Oh my God! Did you get all of that off-screen information, General Exposition?

General Exposition *enters.*

General Exposition (*in one breath or dramatically*)   So, you're saying that Jane Blonde discovered Mr Lovely's Lovely Wellness Resort is a front for EVIW HQ and has discovered a secret and very suspicious-looking clifftop facility, but whilst climbing the cliff to investigate the suspicious-looking clifftop facility her rope mysteriously snapped, leaving her in a breathtaking and quite literal –

He takes a breath.

MMM   Get a move on!

General Exposition   Cliffhanger!

MMM   Exactly. And now that we're all up to speed, I propose that we strap in and get this top-secret mission back on the road. All those in favour say 'aye'.

The cast behind the curtain place several hats on **General Exposition***'s head after each aye.*

Producer   Aye aye aye aye aye aye aye.

MMM   Unanimous decision. Good. So . . . What the hell happened next?

Music spike.

CLIFFHANGER! (PART TWO)

INT. TREATMENT ROOM – NIGHT.

Flemish   I must say, Mr Jubbly, that was one of the best massages I've ever had. Things got a little strange in the middle with the screaming and the fruit, but when I eventually passed out, it was all very agreeable.

Jubbly   Excellent, now pop your trousers off. It's time for the colonic!

Writer   Not that cliffhanger!

EXT. CLIFF – NIGHT.

Thunderbolt and lightning. **Blonde** *hangs from the cliff.*

Blonde   Sir? Can you hear me? Sir?

Lust (*off*)   You look like you need a hand.

A figure emerges, **Randy Lust**. *He helps her up, and they face off.*

Lust   Jane Blonde, secret agent.

Blonde   Randy Lust, secret double agent. I haven't seen you since we worked together in Greenland on the case of the three illegal oil rigs.

Lust   Well, well, well.

Blonde   That's the one. I'm here to find Flemish's manuscript, which I think is hidden in this top-secret evil lab.

Randy Lust   A top-secret EVIW lab? We've got to get in. Damn! They close to the public at five, and now the only way in is down this . . .

A shaft appears.

Randy Lust   . . . ventilation shaft. But we'd better hurry.

Blonde   Why?

Lust   Because the shaft closes to the public at six.

Blonde   Just help lower me down. And no funny business, Randy.

Randy Lust   There's nothing funny about Randy Lust.

Blonde *prepares to rappel down the shaft.*

Randy Lust   OK, Blonde, I'm going to start lowering you down.

INT. LIFT SHAFT – NIGHT.

Music. **Lust** *begins to lower* **Blonde** *down the shaft.*

Lust   Alright, Blonde, you're halfway down. Now all you have to do is avoid the deadly lasers.

Blonde   Lasers?

The first laser appears. **Blonde** *dodges it.*

Lust Well done, Blonde. All you have to do now is avoid the second set of deadly lasers.

Blonde *avoids more lasers.*

Lust Nice work; here comes the final set of lasers!

The **Producer** *enters, going wild with the lasers. He stops and sets up the final set. She steps through.*

Lust Easy peasy laser beamy. Hurry. I'll be here. Just tug three times, and I'll come . . . to pull you off . . . the floor . . . really quickly.

INT. TOP SECRET EVIW LAB – NIGHT.

Scientist One (*off*) It looks like Totally Deadly Virus Number 4 is finally ready!

Two **Scientists** *enter.*

Scientist Two Excellent. Totally Deadly Virus Number 4 is our crowning achievement! And I love the name – it's so original.

Scientist One But you know, when I joined Mr Lovely's Lovely Scientific Research Division, I didn't envision us making a deadly life-sapping formula.

Scientist Two What did you envision?

Scientist One I don't know. Something lovely.

Scientist Two You did some great work on that brainwashing machine!

Scientist One Did I? All we ever did was convince some mice that they didn't like cheese. Even that was cheating because we gave them Edam.

Scientist Two I'm sure Totally Deadly Virus Number 4 is perfectly innocent in the right hands. And Mr Lovely is the right hands. He's called Lovely, for Pete's sake!

Pete *enters.*

Pete   Yes?

Scientist Two   Go away, Pete.

Pete   Okay.

Pete *exits.*

Scientist One   You're right, I'm overthinking it again.

Scientist Two   Now, come on. We'd better get back to loading Totally Deadly Virus Number 4 into the intercontinental ballistic missiles.

Scientist One   Wait, wait, wait. Did you say intercontinental ballistic missiles?

Scientist Two   That's right! Isn't it, Pete?

Nothing.

Scientist Two   Pete!

Pete *appears, visibly flustered.*

Pete   Yep, that's right!

Scientist One   What were you doing, Pete?

Pete   Nothing.

Scientist Two   Go away, Pete.

Pete *exits.*

Scientist Two   And once we're finished, we can have an ice cream on the Great Pyramid of Giza to celebrate. But we mustn't eat them too quickly, we wouldn't want to spoil our lunch!

Scientist One   I know. Remember last time? I wolfed it down, got that awful brain thing.

Scientist Two   What was that called? Brain –

Scientist One   Brain –

Blonde *jumps from her hiding place.*

Blonde   Freeze!

Scientist One   That was it, ah!

Scientist Two   Who are you?

Blonde   The name's Blonde, J –

Scientist One   Jane Blonde, we've met. I was working for the North Koreans. You saved us from the amnesia compound we were creating.

Blonde   I don't recall.

Scientist One   So it worked, then!

Blonde   Lovely plans to use your virus to wipe out humanity.

Scientist One   Totally Deadly Virus Number 4? No!

Scientist Two   I never would have guessed that.

Blonde   Where are the intercontinental ballistic missiles being sent?

Scientist One   We were told to send them to a location in this manuscript we received this morning.

Blonde   Written by Ian Flemish?

Scientist Two   That's the one!

Scientist One   Here you are. Inside is the location of where the intercontinental ballistic missiles are being sent and the codes to disarm them. Everything is on page number –

Lust *appears.*

Lust   Bang! Bang!

They both fall out of sight.

Blonde   Why did you shoot them?

Lust   They were evil scientists working on an evil plan for EVIW!

Blonde   Now we may never know where the intercontinental ballistic missiles were being sent!

Lust   Someone's coming!

He exits.

Blonde   Lust, stop! For Pete's sake!

Pete *appears.*

Pete   Jane Blonde, I thought it was you!

Blonde   No, Pete!

Pete   I have to tell you something –

Lust *grabs* **Pete**.

Blonde   Pete!

Lust   Bang!

Pete   UGH!

Pete *dies.* **Lust** *re-enters.*

Lust   That was a close one!

Scientist Four   Jane Blonde, it is you! I want to help –

Lust   BANG!

Scientist Five   I've just discovered time travel!

Lust   BANG!

Scientist Six   Agent Blonde, the codes are on page number –

Lust   BANG!

Scientist Five   I've just discovered time travel!

Lust   BANG! BANG!

He unloads another burst of machine gun fire into the scientist.

Blonde (*over the gunfire*)   STOP SHOOTING THE
SCIENTISTS!

Another **Scientist** *enters.* **Lust** *shoots them.*

Scientist Seven   Jane Blonde, you're here! I need to tell
you –

Lust   BANG! /

Blonde   / DON'T –

Lust *stops shooting.*

Lust   What?

Blonde   – SHOOT THE SCIENTISTS!

Lust   Got it! I'll shoot the scientists!

Scientist Five   Time travel isn't worth it!

Another **Scientist** *enters.* **Lust** *shoots them. BANG!*

Lust   That's the last of them.

Another **Scientist** *enters.* **Lust** *shoots them.*

Scientist Nine   Oh, humanity!

Lust   BANG! How's that for a science lesson?

Blonde   I'm sending a signal to HQ. We need to warn them.

INT. MI6 HQ – NIGHT.

MMM *and* **Private** *appear.*

Private   We're receiving a message from Blonde, sir.

Blonde *makes a very long series of beeps.*

MMM   What does it say?

The **Private** *repeats the sequence exactly as before.*

MMM   Oh my God.

INT. TOP SECRET EVIW LAB – NIGHT.

Blonde   We need to get out of here and find Flemish.

Lust *moves back to the rope and tugs it. Nothing happens.*

Blonde   What are you doing?

Lust   Three tugs. That's the signal for me to pull us back up.

He tugs another three times. Nothing happens.

They tie up **Blonde**.

Lust   Nope. It must be broken.

Lovely *and* **Jubbly** *appear.*

Lust   Lovely, Jubbly.

Blonde   This is no time to celebrate, we've just been caught.

Lovely   You were warned that this area was out of bounds. Jubbly, get Flemish!

Jubbly *exits.*

Lovely   Randy Lust, secret double agent. Good to see you, old friend.

Lovely *and* **Lust** *shake hands.* **Lust** *ties up* **Blonde**.

Lust   Good to see you, Blonde.

Blonde   I always had you for a rat, but not a mole.

Lust   This mole's gotta roll. See you at the end of the world. Can't wait!

He exits.

Blonde   You'll never get away with this, Lovely.

Lovely   We'll see about that.

Jubbly *enters with* **Flemish**.

Jubbly   Found him, sir. We caught him sniffing around the colonic irrigation room.

Blonde   I told you to stay out of trouble.

Flemish   Blonde, be careful . . . It turns out Lovely is a really nasty guy!

Lovely   I am, Mr Flemish, but don't worry, you won't be harmed.

Jubbly *smacks* **Flemish**. **Lovely** *glares.*

Jubbly   Sorry.

Lovely   From this moment, you won't be harmed. After all, I am your greatest fan. I have used your plots to inspire my own plans.

Flemish   That's abhorrent!

Jubbly   Bless you.

Lovely   If only Agent Blonde here were as adept as your hero, the great Dick Hardwood. I base all of my evil plans on your novels, Mr Flemish! I adore Dick. In fact, my next plan was inspired by *Deeppussy*, your finest work to date. Perhaps you'd sign my copy? I have it right here.

Blonde   Flemish, don't let him flatter you.

Lovely   But now I hear you intended on finishing the Dick Hardwood series.

Flemish   Yes, that's right.

Lovely   He cannot die, Mr Flemish. Too many people in the world need Dick!

Actress   Jesus.

Lovely   And now that I have you and your Dick safely in my hands –

Actress   I'm so sorry, Gary.

Lovely   You will write more stories to provide me with my evil plans for years to come.

Flemish   I'll never do work for you, Lovely. You can't make me.

Lovely   Is that so? Perhaps I can tempt you with a lovely ripe pineapple!

He produces a pineapple. Nothing happens.

Flemish   Thank you, but I don't work for fruit.

Jubbly *whispers in his ear.*

Lovely   Oh, for God's sake, why didn't you tell me we'd changed the trigger word? Now I look like an idiot with a pineapple.

Jubbly *whispers in his ear.*

Lovely   Where the hell am I going to get a watermelon?

A noise. **Flemish** *stiffens. He is hypnotised.*

Flemish   What would you like your new novel to be called, sir?

Lovely   How about 'The Total Destruction of Mankind'! Take him away!

Jubbly *takes* **Flemish** *off.*

Blonde   And what about me? Do you expect me to talk?

Lovely   No, Blonde, I expect you to die. You see, the floor you are stood on is, in fact, a trap door that leads down into the depths of the island through an electrified slide, a 10G centrifuge, a maze of deadly lasers, a pit of hungry alligators, a ring of fire and then your lifeless body will be frozen and displayed as a beacon of light for all evildoers!

Nothing happens.

The **Producer** *re-enters. The* **Writer** *looks at him.*

Jubbly   But due to budgetary restrictions, all of that will happen in the dark!

Blackout.

INT. MR LOVELY'S LOVELY DEATH TRAP – NIGHT.

In a series of vignettes, **Blonde** *battles a death trap. Finally, she emerges and brushes herself down, removing a piranha from her pocket.*

Blonde   Next time, I'll go full board.

The **Writer**'s *hand appears with an alternative line.*

Writer   Nope. Try this line.

The **Writer**'s *hand appears with another line.*

Blonde   Next time, I'll go all-inclusive.

Writer   Nope. Try this.

The **Writer**'s *hand appears with another line.*

Blonde   After this holiday, I'm going to need a holiday.

The **Stuntman**'s *hand appears and passes* **Blonde** *a note.*

Blonde   Fancy a drink after the show? I'd love to get to know you better.

The **Actress** *looks at the* **Stuntman**. *Lights.*

INT. MI6 HQ – DAY.

MI6 HQ. **MMM** *appears at the desk, surrounded by phones. One starts to ring.*

MMM   Good God, the emergency line!

He picks up.

MI6 headquarters. (*Pause.*) Sorry – wrong line!

He hangs up.

MI6 Headquarters. (*Pause.*) Yes, I do want to purchase payment protection insurance. I'll call you back.

He puts the phone down and picks up another phone.

MI6 headquarters. (*Pause.*) Yes, Mother, I'll see you Sunday. I'm bringing crumble. No, Mother, she left me again.

He puts the phone down and picks up another phone.

MI6 headquarters.

Blonde *appears.*

Blonde   Sir, can you hear me?

MMM   That's the badger!

Blonde   Excuse me?

MMM   Loud and clear, Blonde! Sorry about the wait.

Blonde   Couldn't find the emergency line?

MMM   Where the hell have you been? You were supposed to report hours ago.

Blonde   Sorry, sir, I've been a little tied up. I need to talk to you about the mole.

MMM   Oh! The doctors say it's good news. I've got six months to live!

Blonde   Is that good news?

MMM   It's 1950 something, and I'm in my sixties, so I'm practically living on borrowed time already.

Blonde   I meant the one at MI6.

MMM   Oh, yes. We think it's probably coming from across the pond.

Blonde   It was a CIA agent working for EVIW as a double agent.

MMM   Who?

Blonde   Randy Lust, secret double agent.

MMM   I never would have guessed.

Blonde   What do you know about *Deeppussy*?

MMM   That's a bit of a personal question, Blonde.

Blonde   No, the Ian Flemish novel. We were chasing the wrong book! I think the key to Lovely's evil plan might be in *Deeppussy*.

MMM   Why can't you just ask Flemish?

Blonde   He's been kidnapped.

MMM   Right, *Deeppussy*. I'm looking it up now. Do I want safe search off or –

Blonde   On!

MMM   Here we are. 'Agent Dick Hardwood dives deep into the depths in a pussycat-shaped submarine armed with intercontinental ballistic missiles equipped with Totally Deadly Virus Number 4, capable of wiping out all non-evil life on earth.'

Blonde   Has there been any suspicious activity on sonar recently?

MMM   I've got one of our top men on it. 007. He's tracked down a lovely lady, and he's pumping her for information.

Blonde   I'm on my own, then.

MMM   Looks like it. Good luck, Blonde. If you need me, call me. Any time, day or night. Just not after five or on the weekends.

EXT. EVIW SUBMARINE – DAY.

EVIW submarine check-in. Above the water, a **Steward** *checks the villains in.*

Voiceover   Welcome to EVIW submarine check-in. Please ensure all weapons of mass destruction are stored safely in overhead bins.

An EVIW **Steward** *enters, followed by* **Blonde** *who hides. The* **Steward** *references the people already aboard the EVIW* *submarine. Usually two topical evildoers and one joke. Thank you very much, Mr . . . Mr . . . and Mr Clarkson. Anyone else for EVIW submarine check-in?*

Mr Claphands *enters.*

Steward   Ah Mr Clamphands, hope you don't mind if we forgoe shaking hands.

Mr Oddhat *enters.*

Steward   Mr Oddhat, hat looking odd as ever.

Blonde   It looks like a gathering of all the world's most evil villians, but some of them are missing.

A final topical evil person enters . . . Liz Truss, Donald Trump, J.K. Rowling, etc.

Blonde   Nope, they're all here.

There is a noise. The **Steward** *exits, closing the door behind him.* **Blonde** *tries to open it.*

Blonde   Damn!

Flemish *appears at a porthole.*

Flemish   Blonde! You're alive!

Blonde   How did you slip your guards?

Flemish   I haven't. This is the submarine toilet porthole.

Jubbly *appears in an adjacent porthole.* **Blonde** *ducks out of view.*

Jubbly   Mr Flemish, who were you talking to?

Flemish   Oh, nobody, just enjoying the view.

Jubbly   Well, get a move on. It's nearly time for Mr Lovely's evil speech, and you're causing a queue.

Flemish   Sorry! (*To* **Blonde**.) How are you going to get inside?

Blonde   The hatch is sealed. Can you unlock it?

Flemish   No, Jubbly is watching me like a hawk. Wait, in my novel *Deeppussy*, agent Dick Hardwood was able to enter the submarine via the missile tubes.

Jubbly   Hurry up, Flemish!

Flemish   Mr Jubbly, do they have missile tubes on this submarine?

Jubbly   Of course we do! Why, what are you doing in there?

Flemish   Nothing! (*To* **Blonde**.) Quick, Blonde, get to the missile tubes before we submerge.

Blonde   Good work, Flemish. I'll meet you on the inside.

A siren begins to sound.

Voiceover   Submerging, submerging.

Flemish   Blonde!

Blonde   Don't worry, I'll think of something.

Scuba Instructor (*off*)   Scuba lessons! Get your scuba lessons.

Blonde *grabs a scuba mask and dives in as the submarine descends into the water.*

EXT. UNDERWATER – DAY.

Blonde *pursues the submarine underwater. During this sequence, puppets, Barbie dolls and movement are used to show the chase. She faces a new obstacle each time she closes in on the sub: a whirlpool, a puffer fish, a giant squid, a fishing net and a shark. She defeats the shark, rides it toward the sub and enters via the missile tube into –*

INT. EVIW SUBMARINE – DAY.

Jubbly (*off*)   This way for Mr Lovelys evil speech!

Rapturous applause. **Mr Lovely** *appears, followed by* **Jubbly** *and* **Flemish**. **Blonde**, *now in disguise as an EVIW Henchman, observes the speech.*

Lovely   Evil members of EVIW, welcome aboard my EVIW submarine. As we navigate the globe, we will launch Totally Deadly Virus Number 4, wiping out all non-evil life as we know it, leaving only EVIW. Now, relax and enjoy the onboard entertainment. This evening, we have a special performance by our favourite evildoer, Rod Stewart!

Flemish   You really are evil, Lovely.

Lovely   Now you see, Mr Flemish, my grand plan. A world full of EVIW.

Jubbly   Lovely.

Lovely   Yes?

Jubbly   Lovely.

Lovely   Mr Flemish through the endless novels you will write for me, Dick Hardwood will be alive forever in fiction, and myself and all members of EVIW will never want for an evil plan to foil again!

Flemish   I won't do it.

Lovely   You don't have a choice. Remember, I have control of your mind.

Flemish   There are no watermelons underwater.

Lovely   Don't expect irony to save you, Flemish. Mr Jubbly has created a much more efficient mind control device in the shape of this remote control.

Jubbly *reveals the mind control remote.*

Lovely   Mr Jubbly, turn Flemish on.

Jubbly   Oh, Mr Flemish, you're a dirty little –

Lovely   Turn on the device!

Jubbly   Oh.

He switches on the mind control device.

Flemish   No!

Lovely *hits the button.*

Flemish   Yes!

Lovely *hits the button.*

Flemish   No!

Lovely *hits the button.*

Flemish   Yes! Evil!

He laughs maniacally. They join in. **Jubbly** *takes it too far. They stop.*

Enough! It is time to launch the first missile. EVIW henchman! On my mark. One, two, two and a half . . . three!

Blonde (*as EVIW's* **Henchman**) *explodes the missiles in the tubes. An alarm sounds.*

Lovely   What the hell is going on?

Jubbly   Missiles one and two have failed to launch, sir.

Lovely   Get down there and find out what's happening.

Jubbly   Yes, sir.

Blonde   Perhaps you haven't been keeping on top of your water bills!

There is an explosion as the ballast tanks burst.

Lovely   Who are you?

Blonde *rips off her disguise and dons the blonde wig.*

Blonde   The name's . . .

She uses the well-known catchphrase of a famous fictional spy.

Everybody looks at her.

Blonde Wait . . . No!

Jubbly *enters, covered in water.*

Jubbly She's released the ballast tanks, sir! And she's going to get us sued!

Blonde Sorry about that.

Jubbly We'll be on the surface in minutes.

Blonde And when we get there, the Royal Navy will be waiting.

Lovely Damn you, Blonde. Jubbly, activate the doomsday device! If I'm going down, I'm taking you with me. Prepare to die, Blonde!

Jubbly In seven minutes!

He activates the doomsday device. A countdown clock begins.

A siren blares. The lights flash for a moment, then –

Silence.

The house lights come up.

Pause.

Jubbly Careful, sir, she has turned on the house lights!

There is a knock at the door.

Stuntman What's going on?

Producer It's probably that pesky shark again.

The **Writer** *exits.*

Producer Go away, Jaws! Carry on with the show.

The **Writer** *re-enters with a piece of paper.*

Writer Tell them.

The **Producer** *shakes his head.*

Writer It's Jeff.

Producer   Long story short, I owe him a little bit of money –

Writer   Twenty-five thousand pounds.

Producer   Right –

Writer   And twenty-five pence.

Producer   That was the bailiff then.

Writer   He's shutting us down.

Actress   What?

Stuntman   When?

Writer   Now.

Producer   Without Gary, we're never making this movie.

Stuntman   But we're so close to the end!

Writer   Unless you've got twenty-five thousand pounds –

Producer   And twenty-five pence –

Writer   They're pulling the plug.

Actress   But Gary's here.

Stuntman   Yeah, he'll give us the money! Won't you, Gary?

Producer   That isn't Gary. It's – what's your name? (*Repeats their name.*) I lied. I'm sorry. When Jeff left, I thought you wouldn't do it unless Gary was here.

Actress   Well, you were right. I would never have done it. But now we're so close to the end, I want to finish it.

Writer   He's already started removing the set.

Producer   All we've got left is the space stuff. I bought all that myself.

Writer   The space stuff?

Producer   I know, I know! We're not going to space.

Stuntman   Wait! What about my aunty?

Producer   Stop talking about your aunty! Unless she's a big Hollywood movie producer, nobody cares.

Stuntman   Well, she's not a big Hollywood movie producer, but she is a movie producer.

Producer   You're joking.

Stuntman   I'm not, but she only makes a certain kind of movie.

Actress   I'm not doing porn.

Producer   I'll do porn again. I mean – I'll do porn for the first time.

Stuntman   Not that – they're great. There are loads of aliens and spaceships and fights and –

Writer   Sci-fi?

Stuntman   That's it. Sci-fi!

Writer   The space stuff.

Producer   But is she here?

Stuntman   Yeah. She's right over there –

He picks someone in the audience to be **Aunty Helen**.

Stuntman   See.

All   Hi, Aunty Helen!

The **Writer** *closes the curtains. They whisper, but are overheard on the mics.*

Writer   If we can pull this off, she might actually invest.

Producer   Can we make the ending work in space?

Writer   Of course we can!

Producer   I thought you said space isn't realistic.

Writer   There are humans in space!

Producer   I thought you wanted to make a Cold War thriller.

Writer   The Cold War ended in space!

Stuntman   Hang on . . . does this mean I have to do the big space stunt at the end?

Actress   You'll be fine. There's no gravity in space anyway.

Stuntman   Oh, yeah!

Producer   How long have we got?

Writer   He said he'll be back with the van in five minutes.

Producer   How long is left on the doomsday clock?

Stuntman   Five minutes.

A ticking clock appears. The **Writer** *and* **Producer** *look out.*

Writer   Strap in, everyone.

Producer   We're going to space!

Lights.

EXT. SPACESHIP – NIGHT.

There is a makeshift space launch where the set is transformed.

Computer Voice   Welcome to space.

INT. SPACESHIP – NIGHT.

The cast enters in space suits.

Jubbly   She's released the ballast tanks, sir! In space!

All   Woah!

Jubbly   We'll be on the surface in minutes! In space!

All   Woah!

Flemish   Look, Blonde – an anti-gravity button!

He reveals an anti-gravity button.

Blonde   You need to lighten up, Lovely.

Lovely/Jubbly   Nooooo!

Blonde *presses it – DING!*

Computer Voice   Gravity system failing.

They float up into zero gravity. They fight in zero gravity. After a complex fight sequence, **Blonde** *presses the button again.*

Computer Voice   Gravity system stabilised.

Blonde   I don't think they understood the gravity of the situation.

Lovely   Damn you, Blonde! Jubbly, activate the doomsday device!

Jubbly   Yes, sir!

Flemish   Doomsday device? That's my idea!

Jubbly *exits. The doomsday device appears, high in the air. It turns on.*

Lovely   That's right, Flemish! A doomsday device! Set to destroy this ship and release Totally Deadly Virus Number 4 across the world! If I'm going down, I'm taking you with me.

Producer (*from offstage*)   Get a move on, people, we've only got four minutes until the bailiff arrives. I mean – you've got four minutes to disarm the doomsday device!

Lovely   Prepare to die, Blonde! In four minutes!

The **Producer** *pops his head through the curtain.*

Producer   In space!

All   Woah!

Lovely *exits.*

Flemish   Wait a minute! I recognise this ship! It's designed precisely to the specifications in my novel *Moonshaker*.

Blonde   That one was really out there.

Flemish   If I'm right, that means that here . . .

He reveals a hatch.

Flemish   . . . is a hatch leading to the doomsday device, and just behind this is . . .

He reveals an escape vessel.

Flemish   . . . an escape vessel!

Blonde   Flemish, I'll stop Lovely. You disarm the doomsday device.

Flemish   I can't do that!

Blonde   Would you prefer to stay here and fight?

Flemish   No, but – I'm not a spy.

Blonde   But you know this ship, this story.

Flemish   What would Dick Hardwood do?

Blonde   No. What would Ian Flemish do?

Flemish   Thank you, Blonde.

Actress   Don't touch me.

Stuntman   Sorry. (*Entering the hatch.*) Okay, Blonde, I'm going in!

Lovely *enters and displays the button.*

Lovely   He won't get very far when I have control of his mind!

Blonde *reaches for it.*

Blonde   Die!

INT. SPACESHIP – VENTILATION SHAFT – NIGHT.

Flemish *appears on the other side of the hatch.*

Flemish   I'm inside the hatch. Now all I have to do is crawl along this ventilation shaft.

He enters the ventilation shaft and crawls along it to the control room.

INT. SPACESHIP – NIGHT.

Blonde *pins* **Lovely** *to the floor*

Blonde   Die!

INT. SPACESHIP – CONTROL ROOM – NIGHT.

Flemish *appears in the control room.*

Flemish   Okay, Blonde, I'm in the control room. Now all I have to do to disarm the doomsday device is . . . erm . . . climb this very high ladder.

He starts to climb the ladder. **Jubbly** *appears behind* **Flemish**, *who fends him off and starts to climb the ladder.*

Flemish   Aargh!

INT. SPACESHIP – NIGHT.

Lovely *punches* **Blonde**, *and the button falls.* **Lovely** *grabs the button.* **Blonde** *grabs* **Lovely** *by the shoulder.*

Blonde   Die!

INT. SPACESHIP – CONTROL ROOM – NIGHT.

Flemish *resumes climbing and is attacked by* **Mr Hugs**, *whom he punches in the face.*

INT. SPACESHIP – NIGHT.

Lovely *pushes* **Blonde** *off and stands with the button.* **Blonde** *strangles* **Lovely** *from behind, and* **Lovely** *bites* **Blonde**'s *arm. Throughout the following, they fight over the mind control button, sending* **Flemish** *up and down the ladder in a battle between good and evil.*

Lovely   Evil!

Blonde   Good!

Lovely   Evil!

Blonde   Good!

Lovely   Evil!

He throws the device to the floor and stamps on it.

Blonde   He's broken it, Flemish, you have to fight it!

Flemish *struggles against the mind control device. He vanishes from view.*

Voiceover   Doomsday device firing in 20 seconds.

Blonde   Flemish? Flemish! Can you hear me? Can you hear me, Roger, Roger?

A moment, then –

INT. SPACESHIP – CONTROL ROOM – NIGHT.

Flemish *suddenly appears at the top of the ladder.*

Flemish   It's Derek!

Blonde   You did it, now disarm the device.

Flemish   But Blonde, which wire do I pull?

Blonde   The blue one.

Flemish   I'm colour blind!

Voiceover   Doomsday device firing in 10 . . . 9 . . . 8 . . . 7 . . .

Blonde   It's now or never, Flemish.

Flemish   I know, Dick Hardwood always uses his right hand!

He raises his right hand.

Blonde   Wait!

Flemish *stops.*

Blonde   What would Ian Flemish do?

Flemish   Well, I use my left.

Blonde   Then do it.

Flemish *raises his left hand and pulls a wire from the device with a BANG! The stage is plunged into silence and darkness for a moment, until –*

Voiceover   Doomsday device disarmed.

The lights come back up.

Flemish   I did it! I climbed the ladder! And I saved the world!

He puts his hands up in the air, then he begins to fall backwards.

Stuntman   Not again!

The ladder topples with a crash. Light down on the control room.

INT. SPACESHIP – NIGHT.

Lovely   No!

Blonde   Sorry, Lovely. Doomsday has been cancelled.

Lovely   Damn you, Blonde. Randy Lust, secret double agent! Get her!

Blonde   I think you mean, Randy Lust . . .

Lust   Secret triple agent!

Randy Lust *appears, limping.*

Lust   Sorry, Lovely; it's been a blast!

Blonde   Thank you, Randy.

Lust   No problemo. See you later, crocodile.

He exits.

Blonde   It's just you and me now, Lovely.

Lovely   You may have saved the world, but that doesn't mean I can't kill you! Mr Hugs, get her!

Mr Hugs *enters.* *He goes to hug* **Blonde**.

Mr Hugs   Hugs!

Blonde   Wait. Mr Hugs, listen to me. Lovely has been lying to you.

Mr Hugs   Hugs?

Blonde   Mrs Hugs isn't dead. Lovely has been holding her captive, and she's right here!

Blonde *reveals* **Mrs Hugs**. *They hug, and romantic music plays for a moment.*

Mrs Hugs   Hugs!

Mr Hugs   Hugs!

Mrs Hugs *exits.* **Mr Hugs** *goes to hug* **Blonde**.

Mr Hugs   Hugs!

Blonde   No! Don't thank me. Thank . . . Mr Lovely!

Lovely *re-enters.*

Mr Hugs   Hugs!

Lovely   No!

Mrs Hugs *turns to* **Lovely**. *He hugs him in a death grip.* **Flemish** *enters.*

Flemish   Blonde, the watch!

Blonde *throws* **Flemish** *the watch.*

Blonde   Press the button!

Flemish *presses the button. Horn!*

Blonde   The other one!

BEEP! Muted sound effect.

Flemish (*shouting*)   What?

Blonde   The other one!

Flemish (*shouting*)   What?

Blonde   The other one!

Flemish   Oh!

He presses the watch and it begins to beep, quickly –

Lovely   No!

Flemish   It worked! You saved the world!

Blonde   No, Flemish. We saved the world. Now, get in the escape vessel.

She and **Flemish** *board the escape vessel.*

Blonde   Flemish, will you do the honours?

Flemish   I thought you'd never ask.

Blonde   Just make it a good one.

Flemish   Space pun!

He and **Mr Hugs** *exit.*

Blonde   Time's up, Lovely.

She throws the watch at her and exits.

Lovely   Noooooooo!

Nothing happens.

Producer   Press the button.

The jingle plays.

Actress (*off*)   Press the button!

The jingle plays.

Stuntman (*off*)   I am!

The jingle plays.

Writer   The red one!

Stuntman (*off*)   I'm colour blind!

*The **Writer** gets up and pokes her head through the curtain. From behind, we hear –*

Writer   Right. You press this button when I say 'no' –

Stuntman   Now?

Writer   No.

Stuntman   That's my cue!

BANG! The pyrotechnic goes off. Silence, then –

Stuntman   Sorry!

*The **Producer** buries his head in his hands. The **Writer** puts her hand on his shoulder.*

Writer   Don't worry. We can fix it in the edit.

Blackout. Silence for a moment, then –

EXT. SPACE – NIGHT.

Finally, the escape vessel floats into space. The escape vessel floats into space. The cast enters the stage, puppeting makeshift space debris (tin foil on sticks) and throwing more debris (balloons) into the audience.

Some small opportunities for vamping here. The **Producer** *might reference* **Gary** *or* **Aunty Helen**.

All   Space Debris! (*Repeated throughout the scene.*)

Producer   There's still time to invest, Aunty Helen.

All (*vamp*)   Space debris! Bin bag! etc.

INT. IAN FLEMISH'S COUNTRY HOME – DAY.

Ian Flemish's country home. He is back at his desk.

Flemish   BANG! The ship exploded and broke into a million pieces. The end.

Blonde *enters with* **MMM**. **MMM** *puts his coat in the closet.*

Blonde   That's good. It's much better than that rubbish you used to write.

Flemish   Blonde!

Blonde   What's it called?

Flemish   'The Extraordinary Adventures of Ian Flemish . . . and Jane Blonde'.

MMM   Not very catchy.

Blonde   I like it.

MMM   I'm just here to deliver this. It's the manuscript. I've personally been through every inch of it, and there's no code or cypher to find. I did, however, make some notes.

Flemish   Thank you.

MMM   Lovely's plans for EVIW went down with that submarine.

Blonde   Spaceship, sir.

MMM   Of course. So, Flemish, you're safe to do whatever you like with it.

Flemish *takes the manuscript and moves to the bin.*

Flemish   I might not like to admit it, but Lovely was right. The world needs a hero. The world needs Dick.

He bins the manuscript.

MMM   Well, good work, both of you. I must say you make quite the team.

Blonde   We'll see about that, sir.

Flemish *reaches out to* **Blonde**.

Blonde   Don't touch me.

MMM   Flemish, if you ever need me, you can reach me on the emergency line.

Blonde   Not that again.

MMM   Oh, don't worry, Blonde! We've painted it red –

The emergency line starts ringing.

No more mistakes.

Private (*off*)   Emergency line, sir!

MMM (*answering*)   Hello? Go away, Mother.

Blonde   Seems fool proof sir.

Flemish   I do still have one question: If Randy Lust was on our side all along, did you ever find the real mole?

MMM   Oh, yes! In fact, after the surgery, the doctors let me keep it. My wife has nicknamed him Adrian, and we keep him in a little jar above my fireplace.

Blonde   The one at MI6, sir.

MMM   Of course. Sadly not.

Flemish   Mmm.

MMM   Yes?

Flemish   Just thinking.

Blonde   That's it. Every villain in the world is gone. There is no more EVIW.

Flemish   This calls for a celebration.

He opens the box of Celebrations, they are empty.

Producer (*off*)   Sorry!

MMM   Well, that was fun! Now, I'm off to see a man about a dog. And by dog, I mean an inflamed –

Blonde   Goodbye, sir.

Flemish   And what about you, Blonde? What will you do now?

Blonde   If there are no villains, there's no need for a hero. I'm going to hand in my notice.

MMM   Your notice?

Flemish   But you're a spy. What are you going to do?

Blonde   The first thing I'll do is take you and your new book to the publishers.

Flemish   Then what?

Blonde   Then I think I'll dye my hair.

Flemish   What?

Blonde   What do you think of the name Brown?

A noise. **MMM** *stiffens.*

MMM   Trigger word: Brown. Agent: Activated. Code name: Mole. Target: Ian Flemish.

He pulls out a handgun. **Blonde** *does the same.* **Flemish** *looks out.*

Flemish   Well, that was . . . inconvenient!

The **Producer** *suddenly appears in the scene unexpectedly.*

Producer   So, Gary, Aunty Helen – what do you think?

Blackout. BANG!

The end.

CLOSING CREDITS

As the credits roll, we hear the title song 'Definitely Time to Die Again Maybe', a pastiche of spy movie songs, new and old.

DEFINITELY TIME TO DIE AGAIN MAYBE

Time to die,
You're running out of time, it's –
Time to die,
The blood you've spilt is
Time to die,
You've killed and killed
And died a thousand times
So now it's time to . . .

Your mission is upon your desk,
For Queen and country, life and death,
You're somewhere in the middle.
You're cold as ice,
Just like your drink,
It's shaken, stirred and jiggled.

You know your craft,
You wrote the book.
The watch upon your wrist.
But when you look upon the hour
It only tells you that it's . . .

Time to die,
It's definitely time to die,
It's definitely time to die again . . .
Maybe.

For a complete listing of
Methuen Drama titles, visit:
www.bloomsbury.com/drama

Follow us on X and keep up to date with
our news and publications
@MethuenDrama